A Woman of Limited Means

Eileen Sloan Powell

To Anne,

Best Wishes —

Eileen Sloan Powell

AmErica House
Baltimore

First printing

ISBN: 1-59129-261-1
PUBLISHED BY
AMERICA HOUSE BOOK PUBLISHERS
www.publishamerica.com
Baltimore

Printed in the United States of America

This book is dedicated to Shirley Fitch. As a fellow writer, you encouraged me and challenged me with your praise and encouragement. Without you, the words in this book would still be trapped in my heart. Thank you for being there for me.

Acknowledgements

I would like to acknowledge and give my sincere thanks to the following, who made this book come to life and become a reality.

My counselor and friend, Sara, who led me to understand that my mother was strong, and that I have inherited her strength.

My sister, Elsmarie, for listening to me read the pages, crying with me and cheering me on to finish the book.

My son, Scott, whose loving kindness and support carried me through to the last page.

My son, Sherm, Jr., who reminded me to feel confident about my work and never give up.

My agent, Brenda, for believing that my work was worthwhile and should be read by others.

Foreword
By Sara Terrano, C.S.W

Like many family stories, this is a portrayal of life situated in both the personal and political realm. It is the story of family roles shaped over time by alcoholism and mental illness and then tempered by loss and grief. It is a story over a lifespan… not a moment, and a reflection of how people stand up over generations. Most of all, this. is a story of courage, stamina, healing, family loyalty and honor. It is about the power of a re-visioned life through personal struggle and reflection. This is a story about women and the balance of power in our personal and public lives. This is a story about a woman who was forced to become a "visitor" in her own home.

The story is also about societal changes. A family facing addiction and mental illness today is likely to be supported by the hard work of people who have advocated for legislation and policy that have helped buffer the emotional toll of family members. Today, an employee assistance program may be available. A Council on Alcoholism, or the National Alliance for the Mentally Ill, would be at the forefront reaching out to family members and concerned others. The peer empowerment movement would also rise to respond in today's society. Peer educators play a critical role in hospital diversion programming. Significant strides continue to be made in pharmacology and assist people in maintaining quality of life. The power of secrecy and shame has been greatly lessened since the 1950's, due to public health and mental health education. Those suffering are also supported; by the media and the thousands of public figures who have come forward to tell their stories of recovery. The family IS a focus of services supported by medical staff, as well as psychologists and social workers and there are residential programs today designed to keep children and parents unified.

Readers are encouraged to look beyond Irene's powerlessness over her environment to the depth of courage and strength that she called upon to endure that which she could not change. This is a story of hope and empowerment.

Sara Terrano's experience spans twenty-five years. She specializes in counseling for families and couples. She provides services for those suffering from addictions and offers help to those who are dealing with grief resulting from loss due to death, or divorce.

Introduction

If I can share what I know about Irene Esther Stewart Sandquist in a way that will make her seem familiar to someone else, then maybe she will become real to me. Maybe she'll become more than a shadow gazing out the window of a darkened room, or a soft sobbing that I strained to hear from my bedroom; a sound that was, I later recognized, as deep sorrow. Her voice was strong in my very early years, offering the usual array of threats and admonishments one gives to small children, "Don't you go out without your hat!" and "Don't you talk back to me! I'll give you something to cry about!" It was the voice of a mother who loved her children, and sometimes it was that of a wife in the middle of the night arguing with a husband who had come home drunk and broke on too many occasions, "What's the matter with you? What am I supposed to feed these kids? You're nothing but a drunken bum! What would your mother say if she saw you now?"

Over the years to follow my mother's voice became softer and softer until I don't remember hearing it. She stopped the admonishments and the arguments with my father and became an accommodating guest; a visitor in her own home. Her spirit was quelled by the very institutions and laws that were designed to protect people. Instead, the system worked to ravage our little family of four. Too little state money allocated for the unpopular cause of mental illness and a general misunderstanding of the disease of alcoholism and how it affects families robbed two little girls of a mother, and a woman of her rightful place in her family. My sister and I will never know the wisdom she might have imparted to us. We were envious of other children as they rolled their eyes and gushed, "My mother will kill me if I'm late for supper." Or watched in amazement as other mothers confidently chose food in the grocery store, or listened as they called their children into the house at the end of the day.

What must she have been thinking all those years that our family was torn apart? Did she feel the same emptiness inside that I felt, as the very simplest of pleasures were denied her? She must have. How did she bear it? As adults, my sister and I have searched the family albums and looked into the eyes of our mother as a teenager holding up her baby sister, and as a stylish young woman whose arm was linked with an equally stylish girlfriend. We see laughter in their eyes and smiles on their faces. What were her hopes and dreams then? Did she, like so many young women of her day, hope only for marriage to our father, her childhood sweetheart, and a house full of happy children? Probably. And where did it begin to fall apart? Dad said he took his first drink when he played the drum in the Salvation Army Band with his brother when he was barely more than a kid. Did alcoholism show up that early? So many alcoholics say that their first drink opened up a world they never knew existed before; that they felt attractive and confident for the first time in their lives with that first jolt of whiskey, or rum, or vodka. That tall handsome young Swedish man with the deep blue eyes and waves of thick light brown hair that looked golden in the sunlight, and his dark-haired, brown-eyed young wife were such a handsome couple in the beginning. Where did they go wrong?

There was a nice house on Thayer Street with polished wood floors and kitchen appliances that glistened in the snapshots. A lady was photographed on the porch of that house hanging diapers on a clothesline. She wore a nice coat and matching hat. It looked so... normal. Picture a young woman all puffed up with maternal pride. She had become a member of that sisterhood of women who have borne a child. No longer a longing outsider, she could hold her head high and discuss diapers and formulas with the others. And who was manning the camera for all of the home shots? It had to be Daddy. So there was a time, then, when taking pictures of his offspring was more important than going for a "short beer."

How I would have loved to have known them then! I would have asked my mother questions about everything. I would have asked her how old she wanted me to be before I started dating, and what she would recommend for cramps, and how she felt on her first date, and what her favorite color was. Well… I would have asked her then, if I had known that I would never get the opportunity to ask later, and if I had known how much it would eventually mean to me to know those answers. Now, after running for years from the pain of all of the missed opportunities and the longing for my mother's touch, I can only go back to try to make some sense of it all, for her, and of course, for me. She was a prisoner as surely as some people in other countries became prisoners of war. She was shackled by a time in our history when alcoholism wasn't considered a disease and nice people didn't discuss it; people drank because others drove them to it, and a woman who had fits of temper at three in the morning in a falling down shack over a husband who drank too much could easily be called mentally unbalanced. There was no one to speak on her behalf. No court-appointed attorney to plead her case for freedom. In fact, no hearing at all. Simply a dark sedan and two people employed by the state who came and stole her away from her children like thieves in the night.

Irene Esther Stewart Sandquist was here for fifty short years and during that time she gave birth to three daughters, two of whom survive. This is her story as closely as I am able to remember it. She was stylish in those early days and she always loved music, especially opera, and dancing and good movies. She was a good cook and crocheted and knitted beautiful sweaters, and probably the most important lesson to learn from her was to always speak well of others and hold no blame against anyone for your misfortunes. She found joy in simple things; a delicate flower printed on the edge of a twenty-five cent hanky purchased at the department store downtown. Who knows what she could have contributed if she had not been kept behind the brick walls of the state mental hospital at Helmuth for fourteen years? Years that quieted her calls for reason and sobriety in her home and pushed back her need for the role of mother, wife, and community member, in favor of simply finding a place to be; a place that would offer a modicom of decency and peace. It was a life, after all, even if it was as a worker in the hospital laundry with a circle of friends with broken or missing teeth who also had no one to sign them out. She is a classic case of being born too soon for the world in which she lived, Today, Dad might have been forced into one of the hundreds of treatment centers for his alcoholism; the family would have been invited to participate in a family treatment program. Mom would have learned that she was not responsible for Dad's drinking and that she was not crazy, after all. She would have discovered others who were living the same nightmare who would have revealed their own out-of-control and sometimes violent behavior, due to the frustration of trying to adjust to a situation for which there is no possible way to adjust.

As I go back to my earliest recollection of my mother, I go back to a time when the adults in my world loomed over me and nothing seemed strange because there was no point of comparison. Things simply were the way they were and, as the last of her three children, my earliest memories of our home were in a place where we all lived that came after the nice house on Thayer Street had been lost. For all I knew then, everyone had water from the lake all over the floor in their living rooms. It was in a house that my sister and I have come to refer to as "the house in the lake." The shoreline over the years had eroded, causing the shabby and, by normal standards, uninhabitable condition that made the little house something that my father could afford on his fireman's wages and still allow him to support his drinking habit. He didn't hang around long enough, as I recall, to be disturbed by it, but I know my sister, who was five years older and in school, hated it. What must our mother have gone through in that horrible place and in all of the others that had come before and were yet to come for her? She had survived the death of her beloved first-born child at nine months old from spinal meningitis, leaving her childless again until my sister's arrival five years later. She had come through the Great Depression and had nearly lost my father in a huge downtown fire from which his injuries in the line of duty were bad enough to keep him in the hospital for many weeks. Times were not good for my parents and while my father was drowning his troubles in alcohol, Mom was simply enduring. The year was 1948.

I

It was hard to think what my oldest sister would have looked like in life, because all we had was that picture of a dead baby in a casket. The picture was laying loose with all the others that smelled old and musty in the frayed, brown album. It was bigger than the others; big enough to cover my lap. It was a black and white photograph of a white coffin with a small, still baby in it. The baby's face was mostly covered by the lace edge of a white bonnet, but there was enough showing so you could see the eyes tight shut. Most of her body up to her neck was covered with a white blanket and the two little hands curled into fists lay silently on top of the cover. Sometimes I'd say to the picture, "Open your eyes and don't be dead, little baby! You make everyone sad." Other times she just looked cozy, all covered up snug in that pretty blanket. Even during those early years I sensed that the dead baby had experienced a different life from the one that Elsmarie and I lived with our parents.

Daddy hated the dead baby picture and if he caught me looking at it he always said he would tear it up. One night, he came home when I was still up, and I was looking at the picture. "Give me that damn thing!" he said. He snatched it right out of my hands and tore it right in two and took it in the kitchen and stuffed it in the garbage bag. I went out and looked for it after he went back out and I could see the pieces of it wrinkled up and partly covered with old coffee grounds.

I wondered what Ma would say when she found out it was gone because she looked at it sometimes, too, and she cried every time she saw it. "That's Carol," she would say and the tears would run down her cheeks and some more would bubble out of her nose. "She was your sister. Wasn't she pretty?" Sometimes Ma didn't look too bad, and sometimes she looked ugly, but she always looked worse when she cried like that because her nose would get all red. Sometimes her hair was all tangled and she would just sit and not talk for a long time.

Carol died a long time before I was born. She died before Elsmarie was born, too. On another page in the album was a picture of Daddy holding a baby on his shoulders. They said it was Carol the day she was baptized. Daddy had on white pants and a dark jacket. He looked so different with his hair slicked back, his eyes were clear and steady and he had a smile on his face. There was one of Ma, too, standing all by herself: At least they said it was Ma, but I could hardly believe it. She looked as good as any movie star in a magazine. I never believed that the people in that photo album were the same people that lived with me in that little house.

I was the youngest one of our family. I liked babies and I kept hoping Ma would have another one so I would have someone to play with. I decided I would be nice to a baby sister. I wouldn't ever hit her, or yell at her, or leave her alone. I wasn't going to be mean or bossy like Elsmarie. Then, when everyone went away and left me by myself, I'd have someone to play with. Elsmarie was almost five whole years older than me and she knew everything. She also looked like Daddy. She had light-colored hair and blue eyes. There were some pictures of her in the picture album when she was about four that looked really good. Her hair was all blond then and combed special and she always had on a nice dress and it looked like she had white socks and white shoes to match with a strap across the top of her foot. There was one of her in a backyard by a swing that was tied to a tree branch. There she was, leaning against the seat of that swing, smiling. She looked nice, not skinny, and not mean. Someone wrote on the bottom of the picture. "What's those words say, Elsmarie?" I asked. I was sitting on the couch with all the pictures in my lap and she was sitting on the other end of the big brown couch looking at her schoolbook. I held the album up and showed her the picture.

"It says, 'Elsmarie's swing,' Stupid." She seemed to get mad over the album sometimes.

"Where's your swing now, Elsmarie?"

"It got left at that house with all the rest of my stuff. We had a nice house and that was my backyard and my swing. I had my own

room and toys and clothes and everything before you came along.
We had to move after you came! Don't you see those pictures of my
house?"

"It was a nice house. Are you gonna cry, Elsmarie?" She looked
like she was gonna sometimes. I just decided to go ahead and look
at the house pictures again. There were lots of them in the album.
Whoever lived in that house had big rooms with shiny wood floors
and pictures on the walls. There was a picture of a child's bedroom
with stuffed animals on a little bed. Another picture showed a baby's
high chair in a pretty kitchen with toys on the tray; underneath
someone had written, "Elsmarie's toys." There was also a lady
wearing a pretty coat and hat out on a porch. Someone took her
picture while she was hanging up baby diapers. She smiled at the
camera like she really was having a good time. There were other
pictures of pretty people at parties all sitting around together smiling.
I didn't know any of them, but Elsmarie said they were all pictures
of our family and the woman on the porch was our mother.

Elsmarie moved over to look at the pictures with me for a while
and then she said, "It's stupid to cry! You and Ma are the only ones
in this family that cry. Ma cries over nothing and so do you! You
look just like Ma and you act like her, too! If somebody says to you,
'You've got big brown eyes just like your mother,' you stand there
and keep staring at them like you can't even blink your eyes. You
look so stupid when you do that!"

My face got very hot every time she said that to me because she
was right. I did want people to say that to me about my eyes and I
did stare hoping they would say it. Elsmarie made fun of me and
sometimes she hit me. "Baby! You're such a baby. Now go run and
tell Daddy that I hit you… Crybaby!"

But sometimes she did nice things; like the time she told me to
stay away from the pork pie man who worked downstairs when we
lived down on Second Street. I never knew for sure why I should
stay away from him, but when she told me she acted like she
couldn't catch her breath… like she had been running hard. Her hair
was wet on her forehead and she smelled all sweaty. She was talking
real low, almost whispering, "Just don't go anywhere near him,
O.K? Even if he wants to give you a quarter, or anything. O.K.?" I

15

nodded, but she grabbed me hard on my arm. "Promise!" she said out loud.

"I do! I promise!" I said pulling away from her grasp. I didn't like the pork pie man anyway. I hated even going by his old pork pie store because the smell made me kind of sick to my stomach. You just about had to go by it to go home. You could try not looking, but it was hard because the whole front of the store was a big window and there he'd be staring right at you through the dirty glass. His apron was nasty-looking with brown stains on it. When Daddy took me in there once we stood back in the little cooking place behind the wall and watched him chop up chunks of raw meat and throw it in a big frying pan. It was hot and steamy back there and there was a great big oven with lots of little pork pies baking all at once and a place on top that had tall cooking pots where things were boiling. He was a short, fat little man with some hair that looked like fringe around a big bald spot on his head. He kept looking at me even though he was talking to Daddy and every now and then he would wink his eye at me and grin showing crooked teeth that had yellow stuff caked on them. Sometimes, when Daddy came home acting funny, he would give Elsmarie a dollar and tell her to go downstairs and buy a pork pie for him. I wondered what she would do now that she didn't like him anymore.

Another nice thing she did for me when we lived on Second Street was at Christmas. We each got a little doll that would drink and wet if you put water in the little bottle that came with it and there was a set of blocks that Ma said Santa left for both of us to share. Elsmarie was all teary that morning and she said, "You can have the blocks all for yourself, Eileen." I thought it was nice of her to do that, but I didn't know why she was crying, unless it was because Daddy wasn't home and he hadn't been home for a while. If we asked Ma where he was she just said, "He'll be home later."

Daddy wasn't home lots of times when we lived on Second Street. The building we lived in was big enough to have people living upstairs of us and downstairs, too. The stairs that went up to the floor above were right by our door, but Ma said, "Don't you ever go up those stairs! There's people up there who might hurt you!" So I never did. Downstairs was the pork pie man and another store that had lots of stuff in it. We could look out our front window and see the people down on the street driving cars and stopping at the traffic light on the corner and other people were walking on the sidewalks, but Ma wouldn't let me go out and play because she was afraid I'd get lost. There was a little grocery store across the street. Ma said they charged too much money, but sometimes they would let her take stuff "on the cuff." She said that meant that she could pay for it later when Daddy had some money. The scary thing was when Ma would have to go to the store and Elsmarie was in school because then she would leave me alone in the apartment. She said it was because I didn't have any snow boots and my feet would get all wet and cold if I went out. "Look, Eileen, you can stand here at the window and watch me cross the street and go in the store. Just watch me and pretty soon I'll come out and you'll see me come home. Can you do that?"

I would say, "Yes, Ma," but as soon as she left, I would get scared and hide behind the chair with the high back until she got home. Ma always had music on the radio and sometimes the music sounded scary when someone was singing loud and sad. Ma said it was opera and that I shouldn't be afraid of it because it was nice music.

We moved to so many new places that I don't remember everything about lots of them. In some of the places, Elsmarie yelled a lot and not just at me. Sometimes she yelled at Ma, and sometimes she even yelled at Daddy. When we lived in Celoron the first time, she stayed at Sally Olsen's house so long that Daddy called her at Sally's house and said he would have her brought home by the police if she didn't come home. She must have come running because she came right after he hung up the phone and when she got home, she screamed at Daddy, "I hate this place and you can't make me stay here! I don't want to be here in this stupid house! It's full of ants and the water comes right in the living room everytime it rains. I want to live with Sally Olsen!"

"Well, you can't live with Sally Olsen!" Daddy said, "You're my daughter and you're living with me! We're just living here for a little while anyway... just until we find something better." He was smoking his cigarette real hard, causing a cloud of gray smoke to hang all around his face while he talked.

"That's all you ever say!" she yelled back at him. "Why move? We'll just move to another dump anyway. You don't care! You don't even come home half the time. It's me and Ma and Eileen that has to live here!"

"Listen here!" Ma said, shaking her finger at Elsmarie, "Don't you talk to your father that way! If I had talked to my father that way he would have knocked my block off!" She got really mad when we talked back to him in front of her; she got madder about that than she did when we talked back to her. When Daddy was home, he'd let us say anything to her. Sometimes I said mean things to her, but she would look so sad after that I felt bad for saying it. She probably wanted him to stick up for her the way she stuck up for him.

Daddy would yell at Ma, "Leave her alone! It's your fault we got kicked out of that last place. You and your crazy talk in the middle of the night."

"The only time I talk in the middle of the night is when you come home drunk!" Ma would yell back, "Asking you where you've been for three days isn't 'crazy talk.' What do you think I'm supposed to feed these kids when you don't come home? Half the time they've got nothing to eat. They ought to put you in jail!"

"Well, they ought to put you in the nuthouse!"

Pretty soon, after Elsmarie and Ma and Daddy yelled some more, Daddy would go get in his car and drive away and Elsmarie would go back to Sally Olsen's house. Me and Ma would stay home. She usually cried for a while and then she'd fix sugar sandwiches for both of us and we'd have a cup of coffee.

Elsmarie was right about the ants. They were big and black and they were all over the house. And the lake did come into the house if it rained real hard. It would start like a puddle under the front room door and the puddle would just get bigger and bigger until it came almost to the doorway of the kitchen. After the rain stopped, it would go away the same way it came with the puddle getting smaller and smaller until it was just a damp spot down the middle of the floor. Sometimes, after a rainy day, when the sun came out, I would sit on the couch and watch the puddle get smaller. There was a ladder in the middle of the living room and that's how we got to our upstairs. When the water was in the house, all I had to do was climb up on the arm of the big brown fuzzy couch and then walk on it right to the ladder so I never had to get my feet wet. It was dry upstairs, even though it didn't have any windows and was really hot. Ma and Daddy slept together in the big bed up there and me 'n Elsmarie slept together in the little bed.

I liked the lake. Ma said it was dirty and we shouldn't put our feet in it, but I did when I walked far enough away so she couldn't see me. It was fun to splash and feel the cool water between my toes. There was a long dock not too far away with boats tied to it. Ma said never to go out on the dock because I would fall in the lake and drown. But sometimes, I'd walk out a little ways and look at the boats bobbing around in the water. All of the boats were the same size so that maybe two or three people could sit in them and they had little motors on one end of them, but there was one special boat way at the end of the dock that was bigger than the rest of them. It had a roof part over it and I pretended it was our boat. I didn't go out on the dock if there were men out walking on it. Some of them carried fishing poles and buckets. When they were out, I just stayed back and waited to see if any of them would wave at me. Sometimes they did. It was my favorite thing about that house.

I don't think Elsmarie liked walking by the lake. That was my fault because I made her mad one day. It was the day that the school nurse brought her home and told Ma that she had bugs in her hair. So Ma took some kerosene and washed our hair with it and then wrapped our heads in rags. She told us to go on outside because the fumes could kill us so we needed to get in the fresh air. I though it was fun to have me and Elsmarie doing the same thing. One of the men came walking by and said, "What are you pretty little girls doing home from school today?"

And I said, "My sister came home early today because we have bugs and Ma put kerosene in our hair and now we're out playing together."

Elsmarie went running away as soon as I said that. "Where you going, Elsmarie?" I called after her. I was running fast, trying to catch up. "Elsmarie! Wait up!"

She stopped just by our house and as soon as I got up with her, she slapped me hard across the head. "What's wrong with you? You're so stupid! You aren't supposed to tell people you've got bugs!" She wouldn't play with me anymore that day.

The part Elsmarie really liked about the Celoron house was when Daddy had to dig a hole and empty the toilet. They called it a chemical toilet and it was not really in the house, but it was out by the kitchen door with a wall built around it and a swinging door to close so no one would see you in there. Ma had to nag him a long time before he would finally empty it and it got to smelling real bad so it almost made you sick to go in there before he would do it. He always waited until almost dark so the people walking by the lake wouldn't see him. Elsmarie usually had to hold the flashlight so he could see where he was digging the hole. He would carry it a ways and then he would have to stop and gag so much he almost threw up and then he'd pick it up and carry it a little farther until he finally got it to the hole he had dug. All the while that this was going on, he would keep saying bad words until Ma would come out and and say, "Carl! People are going to hear you, the way you talk!" The whole thing made Elsmarie laugh so hard that I used to laugh too.

Lots of times it was just me and Ma staying at the house. When Daddy would come home, Ma would yell at him and he'd yell back at her, "If you don't shut up, I'll have you sent to the nuthouse!" They came and got her one day in a big car and she had to go with them. It all happened pretty fast. I heard Ma talking to someone at the door, and then I heard her start to cry. I peeked out into the kitchen where Ma stood talking to a man and a lady. They were both wearing very nice clothes. "You need to come with us, Irene," the man said.

"I can't go now!' Ma said softly. I knew she was crying and her eyes would be getting all red. I wished she had her dress on and wasn't standing there in her slip in front of those people.

"Do you have a dress you can put on?" asked the lady.

"What about my daughters?" Ma asked. Her voice sounded funny. There was a loud noise in my ears and I couldn't hear her very well.

"You don't need to worry about them right now. They'll be taken care of." And then I don't know what happened. Pretty soon Ma was just gone and then Daddy stepped from behind a tree and said, "Come on, girls! Get in the car and I'll take you to your Aunt's house."

I never could figure out just who had Ma taken away. I thought Mrs. Connally came and got her because she had a big car and a man to drive it while she sat in the back seat. Every time she came, Ma made me and Elsmarie hide with her in the upstairs room. Mrs. Connally would pound on the door and wait for a long, long time. Me 'n Ma and Elsmarie would be so quiet that I could hear my heart pounding in my ears, but no one else could hear it I guess because neither Ma, nor Elsmarie told me to shut up. The lady would knock and knock. Then wait for two, sometimes three times before she would finally leave and then we could go back downstairs. Elsmarie told me that Mrs. Connally didn't want to take Ma to the nuthouse; she just wanted the rent.

II

After all these years, I'm still not completely certain of the sequence of events that led to our mother's first involuntary admission to the State Hospital at Helmuth, New York. Someone decided that her behavior was over the line enough to warrant her being taken away. Cousins on Dad's side of the family have said, "Your mother always 'acted funny,' you know." I'm still not sure what was meant by the term "acting funny." I do remember her sitting around often wearing just her white slip and I do remember her shouting in the middle of the night at my father when he came in; But he always seemed to act "funnier" than she did when he came in. And what was she supposed to do in those horrible places where we lived? She had no way to wash clothes; nor money for soap. Did those cousins assume that she had a closet full of attractive clean dresses to wear, just as their own mothers did? Why didn't someone wonder why we were living in those horrible places? Dad had a job as a city fireman during a time when many people were unemployed. The end of WWII brought back thousands of returning servicemen and jobs were at a premium. By the standards of the times, our family should have been doing very well.

It's very difficult for most families, even today, to acknowledge that one of their own has a problem; well, not just any problem, but problems that cause others to raise their eyebrows and lower their voices when speaking about it. Who wants to say, "My brother goes on three-day drinking binges and keeps his family in a bug-infested shack." Picture a proud Swedish family who immigrated to America, bringing with them their four children and only what belongings they could carry on the ship. Imagine the level of faith, courage and determination that it took to embark on that journey and build a successful life in a foreign land. I never knew my grandfather, or "Farfar," meaning Father's father in Swedish, because he died when

22

I was a baby. I know he was a Christian, a good provider for his family as a wood worker, and a stern disciplinarian. Dad told me that his father hit him only once when he was a child and it was because he was late for supper. He said he was never late to supper again and he never disobeyed him again. Farmor, Father's mother, died when I was eight and she was ninety. I knew her only as a quiet, gentle and elderly woman. She was energetic and active for her age right up to the heart attack that suddenly took her life. I know that Dad had great respect and admiration for his mother; he never smoked in front of her and always stopped for chewing gum on his way to visit to mask any odors that might be on his breath at the time.

Dad, as the last child, was born to his parents late in their lives. Farmor was forty-six when Dad, her sixth child and second son, arrived. With the exception of one sister who was just five years older, all of Dad's other three sisters and his one brother were grown by the time he came along. His brother was a successful farmer and his sisters had married well and had nice homes, except for Sylvia, whose husband had died, leaving her pretty strapped for money. The sisters, except for Aunt Sylvia, were all deeply involved in the Swedish Salvation Army church. Every time they saw him, they asked him if he was talking to God. Dad always said that they did a lot of talking to Him, but not much listening and that he wanted to say, "I've tried to get through, but God's always tied up listening to you." I doubt that he ever really said it to any of them, but it was a good thought that made me smile every time I thought about it because I always felt like a bad person whenever I was in the presence of some of those relatives.

Dad was certainly the focus of much attention all of his young years. What were the possibilities for a son who was born in the land of opportunity? It is likely that Dad's family had exceptionally high expectations of him. Surely, there had to be an explanation for Dad's failure to succeed. I believe that Mom was the sacrificial lamb, and as the result of taking her out of the family circle, we all were ultimately sacrificed. When Mom was taken away, Elsmarie and I were taken to live with Aunt Sylvia. Of all the aunts, it was probably the best choice for us and might not have been a bad place to stay if Greta could have been somewhere else. Of all the aunts on Dad's side of the family, I liked Aunt Sylvia best. If only she had would have told her only daughter to shut-up and stop demanding that everyone pay attention to her all the time. I never really believed that an adult might cause me physical harm until we were taken to Aunt Sylvia's house, but I was afraid of Greta; she could look meaner than anyone I'd ever known.

Aunt Sylvia was a large woman who had no teeth at all and smoked cigarettes all the time. She had lots of big colored ashtrays on tables in the living room and each one was full of butts. There were also coffee cups with old coffee in the bottom and sometimes there was a wet cigarette butt sticking up in the coffee. She had a deep husky voice that sounded almost like a man's voice and she laughed a lot. "Well, look who's here," she greeted us at the door, "Come in, Cullah! How's my baby brother?" She gave Daddy a hug. I always love my baby brother, don't I? You 'n me, we're the black sheep of the family, aren't we, Carl? And look, here's the girls!"

"Hi," came another voice from behind her. It was a husky voice too, but not as deep. It was Aunt Sylvia's daughter, Greta. Both ladies were fat, but Sylvia was tall and wore a flowered dress and Greta was shorter and wore pants that were so tight that when she turned around, her seat looked like two big pillows. Her hair was short and it was blond except close to her head where it was very dark brown. Her face was kind of pretty, but she wore dark red lipstick that made her look funny and she had skinny eyebrows that she drew on with a pencil, or a crayon. She laughed a lot, too. "Yeah, look who's here!" she said, but it didn't sound as nice as when Aunt Sylvia said it. "Well, come on in. I don't know where we're all going to fit, but I guess we can sure use some extra money." She gave Daddy a little hug, "Things haven't been good here, Uncle Carl. Stig doesn't send enough money for Brenda like he should, and it's been tough."

Brenda, I found out, was Greta's daughter, and Greta was divorced from Brenda's father. Brenda had big blue eyes and shiny blond hair. She was about the same age as me, but she looked good and smelled good too. She had so many toys she didn't know what to play with, but she didn't like to share so we weren't allowed to play with her things unless she said we could. And usually she said we couldn't. "After all," her mother said, "those toys were bought for her by her father and we don't want them broken because we don't know if she'll ever get anything more from him."

I missed Ma while we were there, but I didn't dare ask any questions about her. I knew that whatever had happened to her was bad, because when I heard anyone talk about her, they always whispered and had very serious faces with eyebrows drawn tight together. While we lived with them, Elsmarie had to do lots of work. She even had to keep the ashtrays emptied and fix chicken noodle soup for me 'n Brenda to eat. Elsmarie was very quiet while we stayed there and it was hard to keep her quiet, so she must have been really scared. I know I was. We watched Brenda play with her toys and sometimes she would let us play too, but usually, if either my sister or I touched one of her things, she would put her hands on her hips and say, "You better not play with that. It might get broken."

If cousin Greta was in the apartment where she could hear, she'd come into the room, saying, "No, we can't let that get broken. You know, her father got that for her; I'd never hear the end of it if it got broken." Elsmarie and I were left to wonder what we'd have to do to break it.

I had to go to bed earlier than I ever had before and sometimes it wasn't even dark yet. I slept in a big bedroom, but I had to sleep with Aunt Sylvia in her bed. I had a hard time going to sleep and I always hoped I would get to sleep before she came to bed because she snored so loud that I couldn't think. One night, I had to get up and go to the bathroom. I tried to be very quiet so Aunt Sylvia and Greta wouldn't hear me. They usually stayed in the kitchen at night drinking coffee and smoking and talking loud. The kitchen was on the other side of the apartment and all I had to do was walk through the living room and then through the little room where you walked in the front door; that's where Elsmarie slept on a couch. The hall to get to the bathroom was right off that little room. I had just started up the hall on to tip-toe when Aunt Sylvia came out of the kitchen and caught me.

"Look who's up!" she said in her big voice, "What's the matter, honey, can't sleep? Well, you go on to the bathroom and then come on out and meet George." I hardly dared, but I walked into the

25

kitchen. I had to blink a lot to get used to the bright lights. Greta was sitting at the table, smiling bigger than I had ever seen her smile. "Well, look who's here! George, this is one of the little girls I was telling you about that we're taking care of. Poor little thing. Look how skinny she is, but we're trying to fatten her up."

"Well, give her some of that pie. That'll put some weight on her," George said from his place at the table. He was grinning right along with Greta and Aunt Sylvia. "That's what I brought it for, so you could all eat it." There was an apple pie sitting on the table with just a few slices gone.

I had never seen George before, but he looked okay. He had slicked back hair and none of his teeth were missing. Everyone was being really nice to me, but I couldn't believe she was really going to give me a slice of that pie. Greta jumped out her chair and got me a plate and a little fork and the next thing I knew I was sitting at the table eating pie with them. It was the best time I ever had at Aunt Sylvia's house. George never came back after that and I never had any more pie while we stayed there.

Finally, Daddy came and got us and took us to another new place to live. Ma was back home again. This time there was no lake and it was an apartment upstairs, but there was an indoor bathroom, so that was nice. All of us getting back together was fun. Ma cleaned the house all the time and sang songs with the radio. Daddy came right home after work and we all sat down at the little wooden kitchen table and had supper together. Ma baked apple pies and made me take a bath all the time. She even pulled the washing machine over to the kitchen sink and did the dirty clothes. She sent Elsmarie to the store for a big bar of Fels Naptha soap, a clothesline and a package of clothespins. I watched Ma slice off pieces of the big tan-colored bar of soap with her little paring knife and let them fall into the round tub of steamy water. The machine made a back and forth noise almost like a song and the kitchen smelled like soap and clean clothes. Ma strung the clothesline on the little back porch, and some in the bathroom, so all the clothes could dry.

Before long, we had clean nighties to wear, clean towels to dry off with after our bath and clean sheets to put on the bed. Ma took a really bad old sheet and washed it so she could tear it up for cleaning rags and for little rags to tie our hair up in little circles when it was still wet from being washed. The next morning, she'd help us untie the rags and our hair would be all curly and look pretty. The house felt warm and nice and there was food. Ma made pancakes and fried eggs, and fried potatoes for lunch. For supper, we had creamed potatoes, or mashed potatoes and gravy and maybe a little hamburger meat, or some of those little wieners from the can. She sang right along with the tunes on the radio, even when she was cooking, and sometimes she'd do a little dance. She had a funny little step she did forward, and the she did it backwards, all the while she kept one finger up in the air and kept time to the music. We always had music when Ma was home, except when she was sad.

Daddy started staying away again and then he just didn't come home for a long time and we ran out of food. Ma told Elsmarie to stay with me and she went out for a while and when she came back she had some bread and sugar and some eggs in a bag. Ma made sugar sandwiches for us for lunch and then later she took the flour and the eggs and made us some pancakes for supper. She was quiet; she didn't sing or talk and she didn't care if I didn't take a bath. The dirty laundry pile kept getting bigger in the corner of the bedroom until we didn't have any more clean clothes to wear and our towels started smelling bad again. When I told her about the clothes, Ma said, "You'll just have to wear the ones you've got on!"

One night, Daddy came home after we were in bed. I heard him stumbling around and talking loud, "Irene! Where the hell are you? Jesus Christ, can't you clean this mess up?" Lights were being turned on all over the apartment and then Ma was up and she was yelling at him.

"Where have you been? What am I supposed to do when you don't come home? You're a drunk, that's all you are! My mother said you're nothing but a bum and a drunk! And I'm leaving you! I'm taking the girls with me when I go!"

"Where do you think you're going? You say, 'my mother said this, and my mother said that.' Your mother doesn't want you! What are you going to do for money without me?" Daddy sounded like he was spitting his words instead of saying them.

"I'll get a job! I'll earn my own money!" I heard a glass shatter and I stayed in my bed until Daddy called me out.

"Hey girls!" he called. "Come on out here and tell me something." He was trying to stand on his feet, but he had to hold onto the back of the couch to steady himself, or he would have fallen over. He was taller than anybody else that I knew and sometimes I thought he was handsome. But he wasn't handsome now, with his white shirt all wrinkled and dirty and only half tucked in, and his face looked dark and mean and there was yellow spit in the corners of his mouth. He smelled bad so I didn't get too close to him. "Listen, your crazy mother's going to leave. I don't know where she thinks she's going… you know, her own mother won't take her in, but she wants to take you with her, so you decide… who do you want to be with? Do you want to be with me, or do you want to go to the nuthouse with your mother?"

Ma was crying and I couldn't look at her when Elsmarie said. "We want to stay with you, Daddy! Will you just take us with you next time you go out? It's hard for us to wait for you… we run out of stuff, and Ma starts getting mad at me for no reason."

"Sure I will, Honey." Daddy tried to sound nice. "I'll take you wherever I go, you know that."

I didn't know what to say so I didn't say anything. After that, Ma stopped yelling and she went in and got into their big bed. Daddy didn't have much more to say before he kind of fell down onto the couch. He went to sleep right away and I just went back to bed.

The next day, Daddy came home early and told us he was taking us to the store. His voice sounded a little funny when he said, "Irene, I'm taking the girls and we'll go get some groceries."

Ma was sitting in the little kitchen at the table. She looked at him as he stood tall in the doorway and said, "Wait, I'll get dressed up a little and I'll go with you. I know what I need." She started to get up.

"I don't have time for that. I've got to go back down to the station in a little while. We'll be right back." He turned away from her. "You girls get your coats and go on downstairs and wait by the car."

Daddy came down right behind us and we got in the car and just drove around for a while, then he parked the car at the curb of a street I had never been on. "Wait here," he said, and then we watched him go to a phone booth. He was in the phone booth a long time. We watched him make three different calls before he came back and got back into the car. "Your mother's not home. I think they came and got her and took her back to the hospital. I'm taking you to your aunt's house for a little while."

III

I was too young to figure out what was happening; that a pattern of
destruction for our family had been formed and was being acted out
each time my sister and I were taken to live with another relative.
The State of New York, through the Department of Mental Health,
had become unwitting enablers to my father's alcoholism. During a
time when good people from nice families did not drink too much
unless something or someone was driving them to it, good people
who drank needed good excuses for getting falling-down, throwing-
up, nasty, blind drunk. "What could be wrong with Carl?" Someone
was certain to ask, "No one else in the family drinks. Not his brother,
or sisters and certainly not his parents; Why... that family makes up
most of the congregation of the Swedish Salvation Army Church!"
Picture the conversations at church: Tongues would cluck and heads
would shake slowly back and forth in sad disbelief and then someone
would whisper, "We hear his wife is in the State Hospital."

Eyebrows would raise and mouths would drop open, "No! You
don't say!" would be whispered back. "And he has those poor little
girls to take care of." More head shaking and tongue-clucking
followed by a sad, but resolute comment, "Who can blame him for
taking a drink with all of that on him?"

"Isn't it the truth? I hear that he tries to bring her home, but she
gets so bad that he has to call them to come and get her. She gets
out-of-control, you know."

"Well, someone must help with those little girls... why, he has a
good job as a city fireman and he has to work!" the astonished voice
almost raised above a whisper.

"Yes," someone would probably say who seemed to know. "You
know, his sister, Mildred, is helping now."

"That woman is the closest to a saint I've ever known. God bless
her. She's always doing things for others; never thinks about herself

at all."

All I knew back then was that, once again, Elsmarie and I had to go to another house to live, "just for a little while," according to Daddy. I was still too young to go to school and too young to ask questions, but I wasn't too young to feel ashamed and a little guilty for not sticking up for Ma after she'd tried so hard to be good to me, but I didn't want to go to the nuthouse with her and if I wasn't careful, Daddy might just have those people take me away in the big car right along with her.

"The first thing you two need is a bath!" Aunt Mildred said. She had a way of clicking her tongue and pushing her lips out at the same time. She was a big woman who had thick grayish-brown braids. looped over the top of her head. She wore brown stockings on her thick legs that were rolled on garters above her knees. Her dress pulled up sometimes when she sat down in a chair so you could see the thick rolls under her dress, and she wore a big apron that covered everything but the sleeves and her big arms. The first thing she did after Daddy left was make us go into the bathroom where she filled the tub with hot water and told us to get in and scrub ourselves. She had a big voice and we could hear her out in the hall talking on her telephone to someone, "Yeah, poor Carl. What can he do married to someone like that? ... What? ... Oh, he'll have to get a place and keep the girls because God knows I would like to keep them, but we can't. No, you know Axel's health isn't good. No. We can't keep them long. Maybe Irene's mother will take them. She's the one that should take them. She's their grandmother..."

After the bath, she gave us scratchy shirts to wear, "I guess you two don't have any clothes because you didn't bring a thing."

"We do too have clothes, but our Dad didn't bring them, yet." Elsmarie sounded mad and I hoped she wouldn't yell at Aunt Mildred because she might just slap us.

"Anyway, any clothes you might have brought with you would probably have to be burned. There's likely to be anything crawling in them. Come here, now. Your father said I better check your head for lice. Dear God, don't let them bring lice into this home!" Aunt Mildred made an awful face as she pulled my hair into parts first and then Elsmarie's the same. "Well, I don't see anything, but I don't even know if I would recognize such a thing. My children never had to be checked for such things."

I started to say that we had bugs in our hair before and I didn't feel like we had any now, but as soon as I started to open my mouth Elsmarie gave me a mean look so I would shut up and then she started talking.

"When is our father coming to get us, Aunt Mildred?" my sister asked.

"Oh, I don't know about that," she answered with her lips sticking out again. You should be glad that you're here now. No one else will take you. I shouldn't be taking you in now, you know, Uncle Axel's health is not good. You two will have to be very quiet and not disturb him."

Uncle Axel was short and skinny and the hair on the top of his head was gone, leaving a shiny pink bald spot. He had a good smile and he smiled most of the time. He didn't say much of anything. He wore nice pants with a sharp crease in them and a white shirt under his button up sweater and a pair of soft brown slippers. He put his feet up on a big square footstool that matched the chair and read the paper until his head fell back and he went to sleep. Aunt Mildred made a drink for him that she called an eggnog and he had to drink it before he went to bed.

"Can we have some of that eggnog?" I was surprised that Elsmarie dared to ask Aunt Mildred for some and I wasn't surprised when she wouldn't let us.

"No, I can't make eggnog for everyone. I don't even make it for myself. It's very expensive to make, but Uncle Axel needs it for his health." Aunt Mildred looked kind of mean at Elsmarie.

"I want to call my father," Elsmarie announced, sounding mad too. I was hoping she wouldn't cry because that would make her even more mad and later, when we were in bed, she might hit me. "Can I just call him?"

"No. You need to go to bed now. It's time for Uncle Axel and I to get ready for bed. You both need to be quiet and remember to never interrupt us when we're praying."

Her house had a lot of rooms and I guess she liked flowers. There were flowers on the wallpaper and flowers on the rugs. She had white lace doilies on the backs and arms of her living room furniture. I remembered that we had lace doilies too, but I wasn't sure what had happened to them. Elsmarie said that our grandmother crocheted them for everybody. The house smelled like soap, old ladies and cookies. The thought of cookies made me hungry, but even Elsmarie didn't dare ask Aunt Mildred for anything to eat. The bed we had to sleep in was in the room just off the dining room, but we were closest to the bathroom where she said the light would be left on. "I hope no one wets the bed," she said, looking at me. "You make sure you get up and go in the bathroom." My face got very hot with shame as I climbed into the big bed between rough, scratchy sheets. It felt like there was a lump in my throat so big that I couldn't swallow. The dim light coming from beneath the closed bathroom door helped keep the vines on the wallpaper in the bedroom from turning into snakes. Right after I fell asleep, it was time to get up again.

It was Sunday and it was time to go to Church. "Girls, get up! Go straight into the bathroom and wash your faces and comb your hair. Elsmarie, you help your sister. There's some clothing that your Aunt Mildred found for you in the attic and it's laid out for you both on that chair." The cousin who was speaking to us was wearing a big quilted bathrobe with blue flowers on it and she pulled pink curlers out of her hair as she stood beside our bed. She filled one hand and then the other, dropping one twice. "Hurry now, Aunt Mildred's already left. She has to leave early. You know, she sings with the String Band." She disappeared into another room.

I jumped up, but Elsmarie didn't move. "Come on, Elsmarie! Hurry up!" My heart was pounding in my ears so loud it was hard to hear anything else as I tried to do what I was told. Finally, Elsmarie got up and we put the dresses on that were on the chair. The way the clothes smelled made me remember the time we were allowed to play in Aunt Anna's attic.

"This dress looks stupid!" Elsmarie said softly. But she didn't get much chance to say anything else because the cousin came back. She was sounding all out of breath. "That's it! We have to go. If you hurry, you can find Mormor and she'll give you some peppermint candy before Church."

I didn't know who Mormor was; I knew who Farmor was; she was our grandmother. Anyway, I did want some peppermint candy so I hurried right out to the cousin's car. The hem of the dress I was wearing was way down and I almost tripped on my way down the porch stairs. Once we got to the church, Cousin Joyce parked her car in the parking lot with all the other cars and she jumped out and told us to find the lady she called Mormor because she had to run.

Farmor was standing outside the church door. She was a pretty lady with white hair that was always done up in a neat bun at the back of her neck. She had smooth skin and warm, sparkly eyes and she always smiled when she saw me, but she didn't say anything. Elsmarie said she was Daddy's mother and that the reason we called her Farmor was because that meant father's mother in Swedish and Mormor meant mother's mother and that's why Cousin Joyce called her something different than us. She said the reason Farmor didn't talk to us very much is because she spoke mostly Swedish, but that she talked a lot to Aunt Anna and Dad's other sisters because they understood the language.

When Farmor saw Elsmarie and me, she smiled and then opened her big black purse and took out a white bag with two peppermints for me, and then did the same thing for Elsmarie. Other than, "Thank you, Farmor," I couldn't think of anything to say, so we all went in the church and I sat next to my farmor while everyone had church. It felt good to sit there; I liked the singing and the musical instruments that the people up on the platform played. Elsmarie said most of those people up there were our cousins, or aunts and uncles. Most of them I didn't know, but I remembered seeing some of their pictures in the album. They looked different up on the platform, though, because the ladies all wore dark blue bonnets with big ribbon bows at the side of their faces. They also wore dark blue dresses with dark red trim and they looked almost like police uniforms. The men all wore uniform suits of the same color with red stripes down the sides of their pants and red tabs on their shoulders. I hoped that we weren't supposed to be wearing uniforms, too, since we were all in the family. But Elsmarie said, "Don't be stupid."

Later that afternoon, there were lots of people around Aunt Mildred's big dining room table. Most of the grownup people called her "Mother" and the children called her "Grandma." There were babies sitting on grownups' laps and other children who sat at a small table set up just for them. That's where I wanted to sit, but I had to sit with the big people so they could all watch me eat. Aunt Mildred piled meat and potatoes and vegetables and gravy on my plate. "Now you eat this food all up," she said with her lips still pushed out. "You are very fortunate to have this meal."

I put a bite in my mouth and started chewing it, but I just couldn't swallow it. Pretty soon, my face started to feel hot and I just knew if I swallowed that food I would throw up. I didn't dare to say anything so I just kept chewing. I tried to think about other things rather than the big wad of meat in my mouth, but it didn't work and it just got drier and drier until I start gagging.

Cousin Joyce said, "I would think you'd be happy to eat good food and put some meat on your skinny bones. Aunt Mildred worked very hard to make this nice meal for you." Everyone around the table nodded and agreed with her.

Someone else said, "They probably never get a decent meal when their mother is home… You know, wherever they live, it's filthy. Irene is no housekeeper. I don't know how poor Carl lives like that."

And then… it just happened I was starting to throw up at the table. Aunt Mildred grabbed me and ran with me into the bathroom where I did throw up. And then I was glad to be sent to bed. My face felt hot with shame and I was glad to be able to press my head against the pillow on one side and cover my ear with my hand on the other side so I couldn't hear them talking out at the table anymore.

It was a long time before we saw Ma or Daddy again. Nights I would lay in the big scratchy bed and listen while Aunt Mildred and Uncle Axel said their prayers in their bedroom. They prayed a long time every night. We had to go to bed early and I had a hard time getting to sleep because the shadows looked like big round snakes on the ceiling and they wouldn't go away even when I closed my eyes tight and tried not to see them. I finally would go to sleep and morning would come. Elsmarie had to go to school during the day and I sat on the wooden swing on the front porch of Aunt Mildred's house until Daddy finally came.

IV

State-operated psychiatric hospitals were built to house the insane, or the "mentally ill," as people prefer to call them today. In 1949 in Western New York State, there was the Buffalo Psychiatric Hospital and its adjunct facility called Helmuth, located in the town of Gowanda. It's been more than fifty years since my mother first entered the system, but, as a society, we still have a long way to go in the way we regard mental illness. Unless we've had to deal with it on a personal level, few of us have a good understanding of its causes, cures, or ramifications. It is usually one of the first entities of the Health and Welfare Departments in government to be cut when money is tight and the last to cash in on government windfalls.

In the 1940s and '50s, patients in state hospitals had more than one strike against them. The period of hospitalization was usually long-term and beyond the means of any insurance carrier; meaning that eventually the care of everyone in a state-operated mental facility would have to be subsidized by taxpayer money. Many people are resentful that their tax dollars are helping the less fortunate members of society. Those same people rarely question the exorbitant salaries and expense accounts of politicians, or the often unbridled spending on non-necessities at the top levels, nor the never-ending list of tax loopholes enjoyed by the big corporations. If you don't have the money to pay your way, then you just aren't worth much. Never was it more obvious that those without means are not valued as in the state hospital where Mom was held. Her diet relied heavily on starches, rather than proteins, causing her to lose energy and gain weight. There was no money for anything that might be considered frivolous and for some reason the replacement of teeth was considered frivolous. When simple amalgam fillings weren't possible and dental work involved tooth extractions rather than repairs, there were no attempts at bridgework, or dentures. Inmates,

36

as a group of people who already had lost virtually all self-esteem, were left to lose any vestiges that might linger as they suffered large gaps in their mouths anytime they smiled. A dentist removed two of Mom's front teeth and I never saw her smile again without putting her tongue in that space in her self-consciousness.

The poor have never been in a position to make demands; add to that fact the nature of their maladies that led to their hospitalization and the state has a population that it can pretty much do as it chooses with regard to their care. Clothing brought in by the patient rarely was returned after the first trip to the laundry where it was mixed up with others and returned to someone else. Dresses, slips, stockings and outerware were often donated by charitable organizations and distributed as fairly as possible, but sometimes the right sizes were not available and everyone had to make do the best they could.

The hospitals were full when Mom was taken there, largely due to the laws governing psychiatric admissions and release policies. She was one of many who was signed in by a family member and not signed out again. Usually, families were reluctant to enable their parents, brothers, sisters or children to be released because of the overall misunderstanding of the nature or treatment of mental illness. Fear of the unknown is the greatest fear of all and few wanted to guess what might happen if someone "went crazy." The criteria for having someone admitted has not changed over the years: there must be reasonable evidence that an individual is a danger to himself or others before he or she can be admitted. Someone must have succeeded in convincing the authorities that Dad was in danger of being hurt by Mom. It was a pretty far-fetched notion since the only time there was a reason to be fearful when I was a child was when Dad came home after a drinking binge.

If Dad had been successful in convincing someone that Mom was a danger to herself, or another by today's standards, she would have most likely have been released after that first thirty-day stay when the full circumstances of her admission were revealed. There were so many incidents of people who lost their rights unfairly under the old laws governing admission that strict guidelines have been put into place to protect people. The laws may vary somewhat from state to state, however, all within reason are designed to protect the rights of the patient. Now, after a rather brief observation, the staff of a psychiatric facility must make a very compelling case against release and present it to a court of law in order to continue keeping an individual as a patient. I don't think Mom's episode of violence that involved throwing a pan of dishwater on her drunken husband at three in the morning upon his return after a three-day binge would qualify her as a threat to society by today's standards.

I was never asked, but I could have testified that my mother had, in fact, thrown dishes down the stairs at my father from our second-floor bug-infested apartment. I could testify that my sister and I might have been placed in the line of fire as an angry weaving drunken man clutched his two little girls next to him, commanding their loyalty while he sneered at the woman who was their mother after she had been attempting to keep them alive and well on a diet of eggs, bread and sugar that she had begged from the corner grocer. Perhaps mental illness runs in the family because I suspect that, placed in the same circumstances as my mother on those horrible nights, I would have been guilty of the same acts of outrage, or worse. I'm quite certain that I would have been taken away by the people in the dark sedan. I don't know how she survived. I had that same question in my mind as a five-year-old the first time I was taken to visit her at Helmuth.

I finally got to see where Ma was while we were staying at other people's houses. Daddy took Elsmarie and me in the car for a long ride one Sunday. We went to a big place that had lots of brick buildings inside of a tall fence. After Daddy parked the car in the biggest parking lot I'd ever seen, we walked up a long sidewalk and went inside one of the buildings. When we got in the heavy door, Daddy pushed a button on the wall and we had to stand at the bottom of a short, wide stairway and wait until a man in a black uniform came and opened the door. There was a loud buzzing noise when the door opened. The man was wearing a silver badge and he had a big key ring with more keys on it than I had ever seen before.

When we got inside that door, the man told us to talk to the lady in the window. We waited in the hall while Daddy talked through a glass window to the lady. She handed him a paper and pen through the hole in the window and he wrote something on it. Then there was another buzzing noise and a nurse came out into the hall and told us to follow her and she took us through more locked doors. She had a big key ring just like the man's, and every time we walked down one long hall we came to another locked door. Finally, we got to a great big room with lots of people in it, sitting together in little groups. Some of the chairs were metal, some were straw and others were made of wood. There was an old lady sitting by herself on a bench who was smiling at everyone. She didn't have any teeth in her mouth, "Hello. Hello," she kept saying to all the people, but no one was paying attention to her. Another woman sat and cradled a doll and didn't pay attention to the people who were sitting in a circle around her.

And then Ma seemed to come out of the middle of all those people. "Oh, look how you've grown!" she said to me and tried to hug me. I pulled away from her and pretended to look at the other people. I didn't want to look at Ma because her eyes were all red and watery.

Daddy said, "Let's go find a place to sit down, Irene." And he walked ahead of us around the big room, past all the people who seemed to be staring at us until he found some chairs for us to sit on. "So, how've you been, Irene?" he asked nervously.

She didn't answer that, but said, "When do you think I can go home?" She was crying now and the stuff was bubbling out of her nose and down her face and I had to look anywhere but at her because I was afraid I would cry, too, and then Elsmarie would just say again that I was just like Ma. It was the biggest room I'd ever seen and everything was colored the same: the walls and the floor were light brown and the curtains that hung like limp strips at the sides of the tall windows were sort of brown, too. Maybe people had tried to get out the windows because they had put funny screens with metal bars in front of the glass. It smelled a little like Aunt Anna's attic, but mostly like the bottle of mouthwash on the shelf in Aunt Mildred's bathroom.

"Now don't start that, Irene," Daddy said, "I'll call your doctor tomorrow and see what he says. Maybe you can come home next week."

Ma looked different at the hospital that day. Her hair was cut short and she seemed to be fatter. She had a nicer dress on than I had ever seen her wear, but it was too short and made her look funny. Two of her front teeth were missing and whenever she tried to smile she put her tongue in that place where the teeth used to be. She pulled a wad of toilet paper out of a pocket of her dress and blew her noise and wiped her face off. When she did that, another wad of paper fell out of her pocket. She reached down and grabbed it quickly, saying, "Look what I've got here." She opened the wad of paper up some. It looked like a bunch of pieces torn out of magazines and newspapers. "They're all recipes. I'm going to cook some good meals when I get home." She started sorting through them on her lap. Some had pictures of food with them. "See here? Some are good desserts, too. Wait till you try some of these, Carl..."

"Yeah. That's nice, Irene," Daddy said and then he looked away, too. Everybody just sat for a long time, not saying anything. It was so quiet you could hear the people sitting across the room talking in low voices. I could tell Ma was trying not to cry because she kept making choking noises in her throat. Nobody seemed to be able to think of anything else to say. I started to say something a couple of times, but Elsmarie gave me that look to tell me to shut up, so I kept quiet, too. Elsmarie usually said that I always say the wrong thing so that's probably what she was afraid I would do.

Pretty soon, Daddy stood up and said, "Look, we've got a long drive ahead, you know. And I've got to get these kids back" Daddy stood up as he was talking. "Look, I'll call your doctor and see about getting you home next week. Okay?" When he stood up, everyone else did, too.

"Yeah, Okay." Ma was crying all over again and she was trying to stuff her wad of recipes in her pocket and pull out her wad of toilet paper at the same time to mop up her face. She reached over to give Daddy a kiss and he stuck his lips out and allowed it. I just turned around and started following Elsmarie back out through the big door out into the hall. I could hear Ma calling after us, "You girls be good. I'll be home next week. Tell your Daddy to remember to call the doctor." I kept walking so I wouldn't hear her anymore, but everything echoed in those big deep halls and I thought I could hear her through all those locked doors until we finally got outside into the bright sunlight.

Nobody talked for a long time after we got in the car and got it back out of the big fence and on the road again. Daddy made a lot of stops on the way home that Sunday. He'd pull up in front of a place and say, "You girls wait right here. I'll be out in a minute. I've just got to use the bathroom."

Elsmarie and I didn't talk while we sat there. She was in the front seat and she could see out the window better than I could and she just watched the door where he went in until finally she would say, "He's coming." He did come out right away that first stop.

"You smell like whiskey, Daddy," Elsmarie said when he got back into the car. "Can I turn on the radio?"

"Go ahead," he said, "but keep it down a little, will you?"

I liked it when Elsmarie turned on the radio. Pretty soon some lady was singing about dancing with her darling to the Tennessee Waltz. It was a nice song. There were a bunch of nice songs on that radio. Another one was about sending someone a roomful of roses. Daddy made another stop to use the bathroom. And then another and pretty soon he was singing right along with the radio. Elsmarie would sing too and it seemed happy for a while. But then Daddy stopped to use another bathroom and he didn't come right out.

After a while, Elsmarie said, "Come on. We're going in after him." I was glad to get out of the car by then. My legs felt fuzzy, like they were asleep, when I first started to walk. It was getting dark and I was afraid that I was going to wet my pants.

"I have to go to the potty, Elsmarie." I was trying hard not to cry so she wouldn't get mad at me.

"You can go in there," she said roughly, but I felt like she was mad at Daddy, not me.

There was a big screen door that squeaked when Elsmarie opened it. She held it open and kind of pushed me around in front of her and said, "See that door over there? You go on and get to the bathroom."

The lights inside kind of glared in my eyes after sitting in the dark car, but I could see where she told me to go and I started to run to get there in time. When I came out, someone had bought orange soda pop for me and Elsmarie, and she was sitting at a table, drinking it down. I went over and drank mine too; it sure tasted good and made me remember that I hadn't eaten yet that day. "Are we going to stay here, Elsmarie?" I asked. There was the smell of old beer mixed with smoke in the big room that made me think of the way our house smelled on Sunday mornings.

"No, Dopey. If we stay here much longer, Daddy will be too drunk to drive the car. Come on, Daddy!" she called over towards the bar.

There were so many men standing along the bar that I had to look close to see which one was Daddy. There was lots of loud talking in there and loud music was coming from the jukebox over in the corner. The same song that we heard on the radio about the Tennessee waltz was playing and a lady sitting with a man at a table behind ours was trying to sing along with the tune. Daddy was turned away with his back to us and was not listening to Elsmarie. I knew that if he didn't listen pretty soon she would go right up to him and start yelling at him. I had seen her do it before when we'd been out with Daddy. Sure enough she did.

"Daddy! Come on now! We can't stay here any longer. Eileen hasn't had any supper. Now, come on!" She even dared to take hold of his arm.

"Okay, Okay! Keep your shirt on!" Daddy had turned around and had a glass of foamy beer in his hand. He started taking big long drinks to get it down and then he set his glass down on the bar and started over towards us.

"*Daddy, oh Daddy come home with us now,*" he sang and kind of staggered towards the door. "Well, come on! Let's go."

"Come on!" Elsmarie grabbed my arm, "We better go now while he's by the door. If he heads back to the bar now, we'll all have to sleep in the car tonight."

Back in the car, I lay down in the back seat and fell asleep. When I woke up, Daddy was in the driver's seat, snoring with his head resting way back and his mouth open. Elsmarie was sitting on his lap with her hands tight on the steering wheel. Her eyes were fixed on the road ahead as she drove the old car down the foggy country road.

I fell back asleep and woke up when we got back to Aunt Mildred's house. It was so late that there were no lights on in the house. "Wake up, Daddy!" Elsmarie had gotten off Daddy's lap and moved over to the other seat and was yelling right in his ear. "Wake up! We're at Aunt Mildred's house and everyone is in bed. We can't go in there, now."

He jerked his head forward. "What's 'a matter? What's all the yelling about?"

"You have to take us somewhere else for tonight, Daddy! They're all in bed, here. We can't go in now." Elsmarie had lowered her voice some, but she sounded mad and like she was going to start crying.

Daddy was awake now. "Sure you can go in. Just go on up and ring the bell and tell them that we had car trouble. She'll let you in." There was a long silence and I could see the mad look on Elsmarie's face in the bright moonlight as she stared at Daddy. He just kept looking straight ahead. "Go on, now. Get out of the car. I've got to get back to the station. I don't have any place else to take you."

I waited to see what would happen next and then I heard the door latch on Elsmarie's side and the door swung open. She got out and held the seat forward, "Come on, Eileen! Get out of the car." I did what I was told and started to say goodbye to Daddy when she swung the heavy door shut. I stood with my sister on the side of the road and watched Daddy's car pull away and go slowly down the street until we couldn't see his red taillights anymore. "What are we going to do, Elsmarie? What if they're in bed praying? They're going to be awfully mad."

"Well, what are supposed to do? We can't sleep on the street. Come on!" she ordered. I followed her up the stairs to the porch and waited while she rang the bell. My heart was pounding as the light came on and Aunt Mildred opened the door. She was wearing a big bathrobe and her hair was not on top of her head in the big braids; instead it was all down her back. It was really long. She didn't yell. She just stuck her lips out and crossed her big arms and moved aside so we could enter. "Go get in the bed and be quiet about it," she said.

I started to say what Daddy told us to about having car trouble, but Elsmarie poked me and I shut up before anyone got mad.

I never knew, as that small child, why we were taken to live with relatives, or why we were allowed to go home again after a while, but I have never wanted to leave a place as badly as I wanted to leave

Aunt Mildred's house. It wasn't that she ever beat me, or called me names, or anything overt at all. We were fed well, kept clean and I don't recall being asked to do anything I didn't want to do. It was a feeling of always being the outsider, the poor relatives, and I don't think I could ever have been grateful enough to satisfy her for each bite of food that I ate and the privilege of staying under her roof. I suspect that my sister and I were as accommodating as two children can be as houseguests. I know there were no toys so there was no clutter and there certainly was no talking back, or disrespect from us towards Aunt Mildred. I had no response to her tongue-clucking and deep sighs she gave over every aspect of our care; I did not let her know, nor did my sister, that it hurt enough to be the poor, skinny, motherless children without her almost constant reminders that we were also the extra burden that God gave her strength to bear.

I know there have been many studies conducted on a child's need for love, but I'm not an expert and I'm not here to offer data. I can tell you this, however: I much preferred our dismal living quarters, lack of food and the late-night drunken ramblings from my father to that sterile, cold environment we were subjected to at Aunt Mildred's house. What a difference a warm smile, an offer of a hug, an extra cookie, or a small toy would have made in that situation. The name of this relative has been changed to protect her right to her anonymity even though she is now deceased. If her children, or grandchildren have ascertained her identity from the descriptions offered here, then I offer my apologies for any discomfort this causes any of them. We all wish our parents had been perfect, but no one here on earth is, and the one person who was is our Savior, and He understands and loves us all. My prayer back then was to be allowed to go home, and one day in 1949 it was answered. I hope my mother never truly knew how hard it was for us when she was away because it would only have deepened her own pain.

V

Daddy came to Aunt Mildred's house and got us one day and said, "Come on, we're going home now. Your mother's cooking supper." Ma had come back home, and for a while, everything was back like it used to be. I liked being home with Daddy and Elsmarie better than anywhere else. I guess I liked it when Ma was home, too. Sometimes she was scary when she yelled at me if I didn't hold still when she was trying to wash my hair. I'd be afraid that she would have to go back to the nut house for yelling at me just like she did after she yelled at Daddy. She got real mad if I didn't button up my coat, or wear snow pants in the wintertime. "Go on. Go out in the cold like that, but don't come crying to me when you're sick and in a coma!" she'd yell after me as I ran out the door. The house on Niagara Street was all the way at the end of the road. There were woods beside us and behind us and a house across the road on the other side. Donny Frank lived in that house and I could go out and play with him and be gone a long time. He was a whole year younger than me and he was only in Kindergarten, but I didn't care. He was my first friend. For the first time I could go outside whenever I wanted to and run away from Ma just like Daddy and Elsmarie. Pamela Slade was a little girl on that same street and she had a nice house and sometimes invited me in to play with her dolls. We had fun in the wintertime because there was a little hill where kids were allowed to slide and the cars never went on that hill. We had a small green sled that we had gotten from the Salvation Army for Christmas the year before. I used it more than Elsmarie because she was more interested in her friends now and she didn't care about riding the sled down the hill. Pamela had lots of extra mittens and she let me borrow them when my hands got too cold and she let me use her skis to go down the hill. I loved to go down the hill on skis and I begged Daddy to get me some for Christmas. I did get ski poles that year,

45

and a pair of barrettes for my hair. I asked Daddy why Santa Claus brought so many toys for Donny Frank and why he didn't bring me much, especially I wondered why I got ski poles, but no skis to go with them. It was late and Daddy had been out. He halfway fell onto the couch next to me.

"Ya know," he said, his voice so thick even I could hardly understand him, "I do all the work and who gets all the glory? Santa Claus."

"What do you mean... you do all the work, Daddy?"

"I'm Santa Claus... Me! I'm the one who buys the Christmas presents. I should get the credit. Not some old bastard in a red suit!" His voice had that thick sound and I knew he wouldn't be awake much longer.

"You mean you bought the barrettes and the ski poles?" I asked. "Why didn't you get the skis, Daddy? The poles are nice, but they don't work without skis."

"You want this! Your sister wants that! I'm not made of money!" He tried to get up from the couch, but fell back down; on the third try he made it.

"I'm sorry, Daddy! Please don't be mad. Sit back down here with me." I liked sitting here with him all by ourselves. Ma and Elsmarie were asleep.

"Aw nuts!" he said. "I'm going to bed!" And he staggered off and fell onto the bed.

Ma was home for a long time while we lived on Niagara Street. Elsmarie wasn't afraid of her and she'd yell right back at Ma, if she said anything to her. I got so I would yell back too. "You can't tell me what to do! I'll tell Daddy and he'll send you back to the nuthouse if you yell at me!" She was trying to knit a pink sweater for me, and one time I got mad at her and unravelled all of her knitting. Another time she went downtown by herself and after a couple of hours she came back with a big smile and a large brown bag.

"What's in the bag, Ma?" I asked, trying to reach up to pull down a corner so I could see.

Ma's face was pink, partly from the cold outside, but also because she was excited. She pulled something out that looked kind of fluffy and had a nice warm brown color. "Look," she said, "I got you this snowsuit at the Salvation Army. It's real camel hair and it should just fit; now you can go out and play in the snow and have something warm to wear to school."

I said, "I'm not wearing those stupid snow pants!" And I never did, either. There was something in me that made me want to be mean to Ma. I hated myself for being that way and sometimes, when I'd see tears fill up her eyes because of some mean thing I said or did, I'd feel so bad that I'd have to go outside so she wouldn't see me cry because I was so sad for her. I just couldn't be nice about anything. "You aren't my boss!" I'd yell. "I only do what Daddy says so you just leave me alone! And if you don't watch out, I'll tell him he needs to have you sent back to the nuthouse!"

One day, when Elsmarie and Daddy were both gone somewhere, Ma washed my face and made me sit still while she combed my hair and then took me by the hand and said we were going for a long walk. We walked all the way to Falconer and Ma took me to the picture show to see *The Wizard of Oz*. It was the best thing I had ever seen. I was tired going home and Ma carried me part of the way. Daddy was mad when we got back because he said he didn't know where we were. I was afraid that Daddy and Elsmarie would be mad at me because I went with Ma.

I was right, Elsmarie was mad when I told her that we saw the movie. "Ma has always liked you better than me. She does everything for you!" She was yelling at me and looking mean.

"What else does she do for me?" I asked. "Besides, Daddy likes you better than me! He takes you with him lots of times and he doesn't take me." I was starting to cry.

"Go on, crybaby! Go ahead and cry! And the only reason Daddy takes me sometimes is because I make him take me. I don't want to sit around here with you or Ma. She's nuts and you're just like her!" With that, she flounced out of the house, slamming the door behind her.

Daddy did lots of bad things, but he did some nice things for us sometimes. He put up a swing in the tree in the back of the house on Niagara Street. It was just a board to sit on that was held up by a long rope strung up in a tree branch, but it was fun and it was nice to have something to do without having to go to the neighbors.

47

Sometimes he brought us hot dogs and milkshakes from Johnny's Texas Hots on Friday nights after he had been at the Morton Club. Sometimes he'd just make Ma stay at home and he'd take me'n Elsmarie to the picture show. Usually Ma and Daddy would have been fighting and she'd say, "I'm not leaving! You go!"

And then Daddy would say, "You kids get your coats. We're getting out of here!" And then he'd take us to the picture show and he'd just lay his head back in that dark theater and fall right to sleep. If he snored so loud that we couldn't hear the movie, we'd just move a few seats away from him and pretend we weren't with him. Sometimes, Elsmarie and I would watch the whole show through twice and he'd never know it until they'd turn on the lights and everyone would have to get up and leave.

Ma liked the swing Daddy built, too, and one day she sat down on it on it and it broke. The next thing that happened was that the ambulance had to come and get her and took her away and I just figured she went back to the nuthouse, but I wondered why the people in the dark blue car that usually came sent the ambulance for her instead of coming themselves. Later, Elsmarie explained that Ma had broken her ankle when the swing broke and was just in the hospital downtown. She stayed in the downtown hospital for a while and when she got back, her leg was in a cast and she couldn't use her crutches very good, so she just had to stay on the couch for a long time. She couldn't do any of the cleaning because of her leg and everything started to pile up. Daddy was gone most of the time and I don't know how Ma got around to the bathroom, or got food to eat by herself, but she was always yelling from the couch for Elsmarie to make sandwiches and tried to get her to take care of me. My sister wasn't much more than ten years old and she was used to looking out for herself so she wasn't much help.

One day, while Ma was laying on the couch with her cast on her leg. two of the aunts came to our house. One of them was Aunt Mildred and I'm not sure who the other one was, but nobody smiled that day. They brought buckets and soap and scrub brushes and they kept making clicking noises with their tongues and saying something in Swedish that sounded like "Yistis!" while they cleaned. They were making faces while they carried laundry out of our bathroom and worse faces when they cleaned out the icebox. Next thing I knew, they had dragged the mattresses off the big bed and the small bed where Elsmarie and I slept and hauled them outside for scrubbing. We had to leave them out in the sun all day. Neither one of the aunts seemed to like Ma very much because they didn't say anything nice to her, and I knew they didn't like me so I was really glad to see them leave that day.

Ma was home for so long that summer that it began to seem like she would always be there. She was getting around better with her crutches and had what was called a walking cast. She was singing to the radio again and trying to do her little dance to the music, but it was funny to watch with her cast on. She didn't care that we laughed and she even laughed with us. And then one day they came for her again. They came right in the house without even knocking. They wanted her to come fast. They asked if she had a bag they could help her pack, and if she had some clothes to take.

"I've been good." she said, "Why do I have to go now? I don't even fuss at Carl anymore. Why do I have to go now?" I turned my head away so I couldn't see her face while they were doing this to her.

Ma was lying anyhow. She had fussed at Daddy. It had been an awful fight. Daddy had been gone for a long time, and when he came in, Ma started asking him where he'd been. "Don't start anything, Irene! You aren't bossing me around! Just look at yourself! You can't even keep yourself or the house up!" The next thing I knew, Ma was yelling and then she threw her pan of dishwater at him. That was probably why he had her sent back.

"Who's going to take care of my kids? We can't just leave them here alone, can we? Please, don't make me go… I've been getting along fine." She couldn't hold back the tears and they just spilled out of her eyes and ran down her face.

"We'll take them for now and make sure they're cared for," the lady said. I thought about the surprise birthday party that Ma had for me one day when I got home from school. I just wished she hadn't let Pamela Slade into our house. I never let anyone into our house. If she hadn't invited Pamela, I would have stayed for the party, but I left as soon as I saw her sitting at our table. Ma acted like she

49

didn't even know that blue paint came off the table and got on your bread when you cut your sandwich in two.

There were two cars and two ladies and one man. They put Ma in one car with one lady and the man and drove away and the other lady started to put me'n Elsmarie in the other car. "Where are you taking us?" my sister asked the lady.

"For now I have to take you to the orphanage; there's no place else to take you," said the lady. She was standing there, holding the car door waiting for us to get in.

"No! You're not taking us to the orphanage!" Elsmarie had backed way away from the car. "We're not going to the orphanage. We'll run away!" I just waited to see what was going to happen.

"I'm sorry, but I don't have any choice. Now, you be a good girl and help your little sister in the car." The lady looked a little nervous.

Elsmarie was shaking her head and she was not moving towards the car. "We can call our grandmother. She'll take us. We're not going to the orphanage!"

"Well," the lady said, with a sigh that reminded me of Aunt Mildred, "We can try calling her if you want." She closed the door of the car and we all went in the house and Elsmarie found Grandma Stewart's number and dialed the phone. I could only partly hear what she was saying to her, but I could tell by the look on her face that Grandma wasn't going to take us.

The lady had just been standing there in the kitchen, and when Elsmarie hung up the phone shaking her head, the lady said, "We really don't have a choice, now, do we? I have to take you somewhere. We all need to go back out and get in the car." She started ahead of us and I followed Elsmarie back out the door.

"I'll run away. I will!" Elsmarie said as she got in the car and the lady slammed the heavy door shut and walked around to the driver's seat. "I know who will take us!" she said and turned to look right at the lady. "Our Aunt Anna will. I know she will. Take us to our Aunt Anna's house."

"Do you know how to get to your Aunt Anna's house?" the lady asked.

Elsmarie did know how to get there. She just about knew

50

everything because she was right when she said Aunt Anna would take us in. It was a pretty good place. The house was much bigger than the other houses where we stayed with people and, best of all, down in back was a playhouse just for kids. There was a door and a window and an old victrola that had a handle to wind. There was even a record to play called "The Woody Woodpecker Song." Elsmarie and I played it over and over. It was so much fun that whenever Daddy took us to this house, that's what we always did.

We had to stay in the lady's car while she went up to Aunt Anna's door. When she opened the door and came out, we watched the two of them talking and then pretty soon Aunt Anna was nodding and motioning for us to come. Elsmarie let out a big sigh as she jumped out of the car and I jumped out behind her. "Things aren't going so good, huh, girls?" She had a very friendly face and a friendly sounding voice. It was deep, but had a laugh in it. A nice laugh. "You come on in and have some cookies."

Aunt Anna had a big sweet-smelling kitchen. It smelled like things baking in the oven and soap. Farmor lived there in the house with her and she was sitting at the kitchen table. She smiled her big soft smile at us and pulled out chairs beside her so we could sit down. "Can we take our cookies down to the playhouse, Aunt Anna?" Elsmarie asked, rather than sitting down.

"Sure. Sure, you go ahead and play. Don't worry. We'll take care of it."

This time Elsmarie didn't want to hear the record. "Leave it off for a while!" she yelled when I tried to turn the winding handle.

"Are you gonna cry, Elsmarie?" She looked like she was going to any minute.

"You're so stupid!" she yelled. "Don't you know we almost ended up in an orphanage today?" She looked over at me from the small wooden chair, "You're too young to understand anything! I just wish I could talk to Daddy."

We were there for a long time and we didn't see Daddy again until he came to take us to see Ma again. She was in a different building this time and there weren't so many locked doors to go through. Ma cried when she saw us and she kept asking Daddy when she would be able to come home. She called a couple of ladies over to where we were sitting. "Come over here and meet my daughters," she said to them. They were nice enough, but it was hard to look at them because they looked sad like Ma. "This is Elsmarie. She's my oldest, and Eileen is my baby."

"Ma, I'm not a baby anymore!" I pulled away from her when she tried to put her arm around me.

Elsmarie said, "Shut up, Eileen!"

Then Ma said, "Oh, leave her alone. She didn't mean anything by it."

Elsmarie said, "Shut up, Ma!" and then Daddy said it was time to go. I let Ma kiss me before we left and I don't know if Elsmarie let her or not, because I was too mad to look at her.

It was still a long time before Daddy finally came and got us to bring us home. Home, this time, was a basement apartment on Tower Street. Elsmarie didn't like it at first, but then she met the girl upstairs and she was okay to stay there. She and Geraldine played together all the time. The house was better because it had a bathtub, but I didn't like it as much because I missed having the woods to play in on Niagara Street. There wasn't any place to slide in the winter either, like there had been at the other place, but at least we were back with Daddy, so I wasn't going to complain.

Ma was home too, but she didn't usually get to stay very long. Sometimes I didn't know that Daddy was going to go get her. I would come home from school and the first thing I would see was that the house had been swept out and the furniture in the living room was all changed around and then I would know she was home. The apartment we had moved to was pretty much like all the others we had lived in; you walked into a small kitchen through a scarred wooden door that had been painted white and there was just enough room for a table and the four chairs around it. Two of the walls were yellow and the other two had wallpaper with pictures of teapots and there were dark greasy stains around the cook stove. The floor had an old linoleum and in places it looked black where the print was worn off, making it look dirty. The next room was the living room where there was a chair and a couch that was so worn it needed to be covered with an old sheet. We had a couple of skinny little end tables that we carried every time we moved and one of the two lamps was ours. There were linoleums on all the floors that also were worn to the black in spots. There was only one bedroom; the apartments always had one bedroom, so we'd usually put the skinny little wooden bed in next to Daddy and Ma's big bed and that's where I slept and Elsmarie usually slept on the couch.

There wasn't much furniture for Ma to change around and I never could figure out why she needed to, but I guess it was her way of showing herself that she had the right to change something. The radio would be playing and sometimes she would be singing. Sometimes the bunch of recipes that she always collected from magazines at the hospital would be piled on the kitchen table and she'd have one out and I'd smell food cooking, but she usually couldn't make her recipes because she didn't have all the things she needed for them.

The first thing she would say is, "This time I'm going to try not to do anything wrong and maybe your father will sign me out for good. If I got out for good I could get a job at a laundry; I know how to do that now because that's my job at the hospital. I work in the laundry everyday."

"That would be good, Ma. How come you changed the furniture all around? You know that Elsmarie and Daddy are going to be mad."

"I just changed it a little bit. You know, to try to clean it up a little. Are you hungry? I'm going to fix some supper in a little while and surprise your father when he gets home with a good meal."

She did make good fried potatoes and sometimes she made pancakes. She used to try to make me eat something all the time. "You could stand to put some meat on your bones, young lady." She would say. I didn't mind having her home at first, but I had learned that the good times wouldn't last. Before long, she would start getting mad at Daddy and all the fights would start all over again.

One time Ma walked out. She just put on her coat and left without saying a word. "Where do you think you're going?" Daddy said as she was putting on her coat. "Your own mother doesn't want to take you in! Go ahead," he called after her. "See if anybody wants you!"

Ma didn't come back until the next day. Daddy was real mad, and he wasn't even drunk. I had only seen him mad once when he wasn't drunk and that was when I was real little and I stamped on Elsmarie's toe. I had shoes on and she didn't and so it really hurt her.

Elsmarie and I didn't have to go live with anyone else anymore when Ma went back. Finally, we got to stay home. I was glad because I got homesick no matter where we stayed, and so did Elsmarie. Some of the places weren't bad; Aunt Jan was the nicest to us when we stayed with her. She always made sure we had plenty of "Mopsy" comic books because there were always paper dolls in them for us to cut out and play with. She had three boys and she was always ironing shirts and pants for them, and for her husband. Me 'n Elsmarie sat at her big kitchen table while she ironed and we cut out paper doll outfits.

The boy cousins were always being bad, and she always had to yell at them, "You wait until your father gets home and you get your underwear off! He'll take his belt to you!" And just about every night, Uncle Gene would go in the bathroom with the boys and you could hear his belt cracking on their bare skin. But neither one of them ever tried to hit me, or Elsmarie. Aunt Jan used to say, "I wish I had some nice quiet girls like you, instead of those boys." It was the first time anyone ever said such a nice thing to me, but it just wasn't home. When we were home, we could see Daddy when he came in at night and no one else said anything to make us feel bad. Dad wanted to know if we wanted to try going back to Aunt Jan's house, but Elsmarie said, "If you make me go to one more place, I'll run away!"

"Okay. Okay. You can stay home, then." Daddy sounded kind of mad because I think he knew that Elsmarie really meant it. She would run away.

So we stayed home and one time, a social worker came. It scared me because I figured it was my fault that she came. She kept asking questions about how many children were in our family, and she wanted to be sure we didn't have any little babies around. Elsmarie did the talking. She said, "Our father takes very good care of us and this is where we want to stay." The lady went away and never came back. I was glad she didn't tell Elsmarie what I said to my teacher, Mrs. Allison. It was just one time that I said it. One of the other girls in the class was bragging that she had a new baby sister, so I told the teacher that I had to take care of my three little sisters while my mother was in the hospital having a new baby.

VI

Celoron, New York, was a place that could claim some fame in the '40s and '50s. It was located on Chautauqua Lake and steam boats carried people from the city of Jamestown to the park, or, for those who preferred travel by land, there was a trolly car that shuttled people back and forth. There was nightlife at The Pier Ballroom where people could dance inside under the lights, or on the deck under the stars in the warm summer evenings to big-band sounds. People told stories that Glenn Miller and the Dorsey Brothers Bands had played there once. Add to all of that a skating rink and a picnic grove for sandlot baseball games, and Celoron was a pretty good place for a kid to live. It was also an ideal location for an alcoholic with four beer joints to choose from, all within walking distance. Dad had lost his job at the fire department and was working for a plating works factory in Jamestown. A man just down the street, who worked at the same place, didn't mind taking him back and forth to work when Dad was a little short on money to put gas in the old car. It all worked out so well, in fact, that the Sandquist family managed to stay in one location for nearly seven years.

During all of those seven years that we lived in Celoron, Mom remained a patient at Helmuth. We settled into a routine of sorts where everyone managed to function on some level. Mom came for home visits whenever Dad would think to arrange it, however, his lifestyle didn't often allow time for trips to the hospital, which was about 60 miles away. The neighbors could pretty well keep up with the days of the week just by watching Dad. Mondays though Wednesdays he was off to work in the morning and home on time. He could even be seen carrying a bag of groceries from Brown's Grocery Store down the block after work. It was on those days, the sober ones, that he usually rode to work with George. George lived down by the grocery and so Dad would just get out of his car down at his house and then stop on the way home and charge a little package of ground meat and some macaroni, or a can of tuna fish and some noodles until payday and then he'd come home and make supper. Elsmarie and I always knew we'd have supper on Mondays, Tuesdays and Wednesdays. Dad got paid on Thursdays and that meant that you could pretty well forget supper, or anything else for the rest of the week unless you could manage to find him and squeeze some money from him before he was either so drunk he could barely recognize us, or too broke to spare some extra cash.

He always got straightened out again on Sundays; that's when the money would have run out. There he'd be, early Sunday mornings, wearing a dingy-looking white shirt with the sleeves rolled up part of the way. He would glance my way when he heard me coming down the stairs, but he'd look away quickly before our eyes could meet as he fought tears of remorse for his behavior of the past few days. I couldn't look at him either on those Sunday mornings. I couldn't watch as he tried to lift the coffee cup without spilling it with trembling hands. Sometimes he'd be in such bad shape that he would have to go out to find someone who would buy him one short drink so he could straighten up. He referred to this as, "taking a little venom of the snake that bit him." I never worried about him coming right back on Sundays when he did that because his remorse and his hangover were strong enough to bring him home.

Elsmarie survived by visiting her friends most of the time; she was fourteen when we moved there and started dating boys. Mom wrote letters all the time, to Elsmarie and me, asking us how everything was going and reminding us to have Dad come and get her for a home visit. I was used to her being gone by then and other than the prayers for her return to me that I sometimes offered in the darkness of my bedroom, I had learned to put her out of my mind. I pretended she was home and lied to anyone who asked about her and seeing as I never invited anyone into our house, no one had to ask me why she was never there when company came in.

All in all, the house was the best place that I could remember living in, even though it was the second worst house on the Boulevard. The worst was a block away from us; a big rooming house that everyone in town called Glamour Manor. I guess it used to be a fancy hotel many years before, but now it had become a rundown place where winos and other scary people lived. Most people crossed the street if they were going that way, rather than walk in front of it, because the smell was terrible and the rumor was that you could get bugs just walking too close. Elsmarie said that right after Dad lost our nice house, when I was still a baby, we lived in that dump for a few weeks. She said a man down the hall kept offering to give her a quarter if she would just let him see her pull her panties down. She told Daddy what the man said and she never had to do it.

The house we lived in was bigger than the other places. We had a porch and a living room with a couch and chair and there was a big open doorway to a dining room where we had a table with chairs all around it and something called a buffet. The kitchen was just big enough for the sink, the stove, the refrigerator and a few cupboards; and the bathroom was right off the kitchen. It had a bathtub and a toilet. The stairway was in the living room, and upstairs, there were two bedrooms; you walked through one to get to the other and Dad broke down and bought a set of twin beds for Elsmarie and me. For the first time, we both had a bed to sleep in. The wallpaper upstairs was stained and peeling off in the corners, but Dad said he'd fix them up later and he really did paint the living room blue, so maybe there was hope, after all.

The only bad thing about the house was the rats. You had to be sure to stamp your feet if you were going into the kitchen so you would scare them into their hiding places. Otherwise they would just look at you with beady little eyes when you walked into the room. They stayed in the drawers with the silverware and in the cupboards and if you had knocked before you opened them you were pretty safe. Once, I opened a top cupboard to get a dish, and one jumped out and almost landed on me and after that I learned to always knock before I opened anything in the kitchen.

But the best part about Celoron was that I could walk to the lake and to the amusement park, and even to the skating rink, but Elsmarie went there a lot and she didn't want me hanging around with her and her friends. I didn't even care that she didn't want me around her because I could go to the park every day in the summer.

I got to know the old man who ran the roller coaster and he let me ride free whenever no one else was around.

"I can't let every kid ride free, ya know, but you're all right and you don't bother me with a whole bunch of your friends about getting free rides, so you just kinda slide by me when I'm working and you want to ride. But don't try it when the boss is around!" He was old and fat and he wore an old baseball cap and long-sleeved shirt, even in the hot weather. His name was Chet, and he knew Dad because they both did their drinking at the Imperial Hotel, which was right in the main part of Celoron across the road from the park.

I loved the roller coaster. It wasn't a very big one and some people thought it was dangerous because it was so old, but I wasn't afraid on it. I loved the way the wind made my hair fly back going down that first big hill. After that it wasn't very exciting, but that first hill was worth everything else; I felt like I was flying. There was a merry-go-round, but that was for little kids. I was afraid of the Rollo Planes, and had only been on them once and they made me so dizzy when I got off, that for a minute, everything looked upside down. There were two cars, one on each end of a big long straight piece that went round and round. And then the cars went around in circles on their own. It was too much for me. There was a ferris wheel that I rode sometimes, but it wasn't much fun after all the time I had spent on the big one that got taken down. Chet used to run the biggest ferris wheel in the world. The cars were so big that two picnic benches fit inside of them facing each other.

The big ferris wheel was where the parking lot is now on the side of the Imperial Hotel. When you were riding that thing, you could see everywhere from on top. You could even see the tops of the trees. If Daddy took us out when he went drinking in the summer before we moved to Celoron, we always begged him to take us there because we knew that the park was closed sometimes during the week and if it was closed we could get Chet to lock us in one of those big ferris wheel cages and turn it on and then he would go in the Imperial and drink with Daddy. Elsmarie and I learned to be sure to go to the bathroom before we got on because sometimes we'd stay on it at the very top for all morning, then he'd let us off for lunch and then we'd get back on for the whole afternoon. We just stayed

59

up there and took turns making up stories to tell each other and looked at everything until it was time to get off. They took it down after that year because someone bought it and took it to France, according to Daddy.

I loved everything about Celoron Park. I liked the Penny Arcade where the fortune teller sat in the little glass cage. She was just a big plaster statue that was dressed up like a gypsy and If you put a dime in the slot, her arm would move back and forth over some playing cards that were laying out in front of her and then pretty soon a different kind of card would come out into a little metal cup. It would say, "You are going to be rich and famous," or "You are going to take a long trip." Once, I got one that said, "You are going to find a large sum of money." I looked all over the park that day, but I didn't find any money.

In the summer, when the park was open, people would come from all over. Sometimes, people who worked at a factory would get together at the Picnic Grove, which was across the road from our house, and everyone who was part of that group would have a tag to pin on their shirts so that they could do whatever they wanted in the amusement park all day. It was easy to find one of those tags that someone had dropped on the ground, and all you had to do was pick it up and pin it to your shirt and you could have a great day. You could go on all the rides free, and you also got some tickets to play some of the games. There was a game where you picked a plastic duck out of the water and won a prize, and there was another one where you had to throw wooden rings and try to make them land on prizes. If you kept your eyes on the ground on those really busy days you might find some money and then you could buy cotton candy, or hot dogs, or French fries in a paper cone with vinegar squirted all over them.

One of the best things about living in Celoron was that Dad could do his drinking right there in town. I always knew where to find him. It was almost as good as having him at home. If I caught him at just the right time, I could get money from him. The trick was to get to him after he started feeling good, but not so late that he was getting broke. It also helped to ask him in a public place in front of his drinking buddies. I would stand behind him at the bar and say, "Hi

Daddy!" And when he turned around, I would smile shyly at him. If he had to blink his eyes a lot and get real close to recognize me, that meant he was, in Elsmarie's words, "three sheets to the wind and gone," and I might as well forget about getting any money. But if he turned around and started singing, "*Daddy, oh Daddy, come home with me now...*" I was in luck.

After singing a couple of verses to his song, he would usually poke the guy next to him and say, "Hey! Look, my kid's here. Ain't she cute? She's the picture of me..."

As soon as the guy turned around, that was the time to ask, "Daddy, can I have some money to get something to eat?" Another shy smile.

"What? You mean you haven't eaten yet? Well, sure you can get something to eat. Here, take this." He'd act so concerned that I hadn't eaten I almost had to laugh, but that wouldn't have been the time to do that. He would give me a dollar, maybe two. Once I got a five. But Dad was shrewd, even in that condition, because he'd be counting as he was reaching to be sure he had enough to finish off his night. The hard part after getting the money was getting away. By then a few drunk men would be wanting to buy me a bottle of soda pop and you didn't want to get anybody started fighting over anything so you just had to kind of ease out the door. I really hated beer joints. I had been going to them as long as I could remember. I made up my mind that when I grew up, I would never go into another beer joint for the rest of my life and my children, when I had some, were never going into a bar.

There were plenty of beer joints in Celoron. The Imperial Hotel was probably the best one. It was the cleanest and they served food in the back room so there were people who went there mainly to eat instead of just to drink. There was a big porch that went all the way around the front and the side of the building and you could go in the front door, or the one on the side. Each side had big, wide screen doors in the summer. There were really two separate rooms; the bar was long and it took up almost all of the first room. There were plenty of bar stools in front of it, but there were also some tables in there along the wall. Dad said that ladies and little girls should never sit at the bar, so he usually made us sit at one of the tables if we went in with him.

Nelson's Cafe was another beer joint that Daddy liked. It was much smaller than the Imperial and it was on the Boulevard, too. It was really just a few doors up from where we lived. I didn't like that place as much ever since Dad's friend, Lee Mason and his wife, Rita, started hanging out there with him. They brought really little kids in with them. Buddy was seven, Patty was only two years old, and then Rita brought their brand new baby boy right from the hospital and there they all sat at the table drinking beer and whiskey and laughing even though all those little children were tired and hungry and wanted to go home. I thought the bar man should have told them to go home, but he never said anything. I didn't like people who worked in beer joints anyway. They wouldn't tell the truth about whether a man was sitting there drinking when his family called on the phone, and they let parents get so drunk that they couldn't even drive their kids home. Now that we lived in Celoron I was lucky I could have gone home, but I didn't. I stayed and tried to help take care of those little children. I couldn't do much, but Rita had a bottle for the baby and I asked the bar man if they could heat it up, and I made Daddy buy some soda pop and potato chips for Patty and Buddy.

I guess Rita and Lee thought I knew a lot about little kids when they saw me fussing over their kids in the bar that day, because they wanted me to babysit for them after that. They lived upstairs over Howard's Second-hand Store and that was right up the street from us. At first I was happy because the idea of babysitting made me feel grown-up. "Sure, I'll take care of them. I know just what to do." I lied. The first night they left me alone with those children was awful. The baby cried until his little chin quivered and nothing I could do would make him stop. I kept trying to feed him the bottle that she left for him and he wouldn't drink it. He messed in his diaper and when I changed it I almost stuck the diaper pin in his side. He had a horrible diaper rash and I couldn't find anything to put on his bottom to make him feel better. I didn't dare try to change him again in case I did stick him with a pin. After a while, two-year-old Patty started crying, too. I couldn't find anything to feed her except dry Cheerio's, because the milk in the refrigerator was sour. Before the night was up she had carried the box of cereal all over the apartment and left a trail of Cheerio's everywhere she walked, but it was the only thing that kept her quiet. Seven-year-old Buddy asked me dumb questions all night and kept telling me he was hungry and begging me to tell him a story. Rita and Lee came in laughing and bumping into things on their way in the door about two o'clock in the morning. They only gave me one dollar for all of that time and trouble.

I told Daddy the next day that I didn't like babysitting for them, and I told him how much they gave me.

"Don't babysit for them anymore," he said, "They drink too much and it's a wonder that those kids are still alive the way they neglect them. Half the time I don't think they have enough to eat. I've tried talking to Lee about it, but he's hard-headed."

I thought about all the times I sat in a bar when I was real little. Sometimes we stayed so long that I'd have trouble staying awake and somebody would tell him to take me home. I remember him saying, "She's having a good time. Look at her, she's got soda pop and potato chips. Leave her alone." I didn't say anything to him about any of that, I just hoped that he would stick up for me when I didn't want to babysit for them anymore.

Dad didn't drink all the time. On the days he didn't drink, he acted pretty normal. He'd come right home after work, carrying a folded up newspaper under his arm. Usually he'd have a little bag of groceries and he'd make us a supper. We'd have tuna and noodles, or dried beef gravy over toast. After supper, we'd clear the table and Elsmarie and I would take turns doing the dishes and then Daddy would settle in front of the television set and watch the news and the evening programs. He'd hardly even look at us, unless we were making too much noise, so he couldn't hear the television. Sometimes, he'd make comments on things that were being talked about in the news and usually he laughed at the T.V. comedians like Red Skeleton and Bob Hope. At eleven o'clock, he'd say, "Goodnight, now," and he'd go to bed. That was Monday through Wednesday. It was like having two fathers. The good one who came home at night and wouldn't let me stay out past dark and told good clean jokes and didn't even swear in front of me. And then there was the other one.

Dad got paid on Thursdays and that would start him up for the rest of the weekend. Sunday mornings, I would get up and go downstairs, knowing that he would be sitting at the table, looking like a different person than the one I saw last night. Usually, he'd have shaved and changed his shirt and he would have cleaned up any beer bottles, or cans and put them in the trash. The table would be wiped clean and the only thing on it would be his cigarettes, lighter, an ashtray and cup of coffee. It was hard to watch him try to drink the coffee because he would shake so bad that he would spill part of it before he got it to his mouth.

"I'm sorry about getting drunk, honey. I only meant to stop and have one," he would say. "I promise you I won't do this anymore."

"You always promise, Dad, but you always do it anyway. Why can't you just come right home after work on Thursday?"

"I know. I know, but I'm going to quit. I'm not going to drink anymore. You'll see, I'm going on the wagon from now on. I just can't keep doing this." He sounded like he meant it, but he would do the same thing again on Thursday. Sometimes I started hoping he was telling the truth, but that was not a good idea because he never was able to keep his promises.

The bad part was when he ran out of money and they wouldn't let him borrow some at work, then he would start looking for Elsmarie's roller skates that she bought with her babysitting money, or her wind-up record player, and if he found them he would take them to the pawn shop. Things weren't easy to come by for us and most of what we had wasn't worth any money. Elsmarie had begged Dad so much for that record player that he finally gave it to her for Christmas that year and now the first thing she had to do when she got home from school was check to see if her things were still there. And sometimes they weren't. If he was out drinking, she'd wait up for him and when he got home she'd let him have it, "Dad! Where's my roller skates and my record player?" Usually he wouldn't answer at first, "I mean it, Dad, you better tell me where you pawned them!"

"I only borrowed them for a little while," he would yell back, "You're just selfish! After all the stuff I've bought you and you can't let me borrow your precious things to bring a little money in the house!"

"What have you bought me, Dad?" She'd look him right in the eye.

"What about those red shoes I bought for you? You just had to have those red shoes!" Dad would act really mad.

"Oh!" Elsmarie acted surprised, "Let me see... you must be talking about those red shoes that you bought for me two years ago. I must have forgotten because you haven't reminded me for at least two weeks, now."

"Well, who bought you the goddamn record player, anyway?" Dad asked.

"We can't forget that either, can we? It was one of your generous Christmas gifts where you come home drunk on Christmas Eve after blowing your Christmas bonus from the shop and throw something in our laps and say, 'There's your goddamn Christmas present! The holidays are just so special with you, Dad. We have to put up with that and then we aren't supposed to care that you take them back and hock them. I guess I'll just have to start carrying all my belongings to school with me!"

"You'll get your stuff back, don't worry and then I'm not buying anything else for anyone. I'm sick and tired of it!"

"Well, don't worry about it, Dad, because I can get my own stuff. I've been working since I was eight years old, babysitting and even lying about my age so I could work in the nursing home when I was thirteen. And now, even though Eileen is only ten years old, she has to take any babysitting that she can find just to earn enough money to be able to buy a decent blouse, or pair of shoes."

"Aw nuts!" Dad said, "I'm not sticking around to listen to any more of their bullshit! No wonder I go out, it's the only time I can get away from your nagging!"

"Don't bother, Dad, because I've got a date and I'll be out the door before you!" Elsmarie was quicker than he was and she did make it out the door first.

Dad was more likely to pass out once he came in for the night, or else he must be broke, or he wouldn't be home. I didn't have anything worth hocking, so I didn't have anything to add to the argument, but everything Elsmarie said was true. I took any babysitting job I could find and I did use the money to buy clothes.

I didn't think too much about how my clothes looked to other people until a girl in my class at school came to our house one day and knocked on the door. I could see her out of the corner of the window and she was carrying something in her arms. I panicked at first because I never let anyone from school see the inside of our house. I thought about hiding, but then, what if she was holding a hurt animal or something? I decided to go out on the porch and talk to her and just tell her what I told all the kids; that my mother worked nights at the hospital and had to sleep all day and no one was allowed in the house because we couldn't disturb her sleep. I opened the door and saw that Nancy was holding a bundle of clothes in her arms.

"My mother said for me to bring these clothes to you," said Nancy cheerfully. "They're good things, but no one at my house can wear them."

"Well," I said, "thank you, but tell your mother that she should give them to someone else because I have lots of clothes and I don't need anything." My face was hot with shame and I tried not to look down at the outfit I was wearing, but I could see that it looked pretty bad next to Nancy's crisp white blouse and bright plaid Bermuda shorts.

"I wish you'd take these," she said again.

"No," I said, "I've got to go in the house now." I went in and left her standing there. I knew it wasn't very nice, but I just couldn't take things from people like that. It made me feel too ashamed. I remembered when I was real little and we had just moved to Niagara Street and I was playing outside. I must have been only about six, then, and the neighbor lady came over to me and said, "Do you have any clothes to wear besides that bathing suit? The reason I ask is that's all I've seen you wear since you moved in last week and if you need some clothes, I can probably find some that my daughter has outgrown."

"Oh, I have lots of clothes," I lied. "I wear this bathing suit all the time because I like it so much. I don't need any clothes." The next day I dug through our dirty clothes pile in the bathroom and found something different to wear.

It wasn't bad if I didn't know the people who were giving me the clothes. Dad's boss would put boxes of clothes that his daughter had outgrown into the backseat of his car and I loved getting them. It was better than Christmas going through those boxes. Most of the things fit Elsmarie better than me, but I got her hand-me-downs. When Mother was home, she would try to get down to the Salvation Army and get what she could for me. So I did have something. I realized after Nancy tried to give me those clothes that I needed something that fit better and was more in style. That's when I started really looking hard for babysitting jobs.

I was finally able to buy two skirts that looked the ones the other kids were wearing, and three blouses. I still needed a couple of sweaters, some good bobby socks and a pair of saddle shoes and then I could just about look like everyone else. Mother liked to buy me things, but she just didn't seem to understand that I was growing up. One time she came home from the hospital and she had brought me some little hankies with pictures of elephants on them. "Mother!" I said, "These are for little kids! I'm not a baby anymore! These are stupid."

"I'm sorry," she said, "I'll take them back." Mother was always asking me about my friends and school and everything. "Why don't you invite your friends over so I can meet them?"

I thought about the surprise party she pulled on me on Niagara Street. All I needed was to come home and find my friends sitting in this dump for another surprise. "I don't really have any friends here, Mother." I lied because I did have some, but I wanted to keep them. If they found out she was in a mental hospital, and that she didn't work nights at the hospital in Jamestown, I wouldn't have any friends left.

VII

The years at Celoron were filled with my own struggle to find some identity apart from my family. I wanted to be just a regular kid and that meant I had to try to forget about my drunken father and my mother who was a patient at a mental hospital. I made up a family in my head. My imaginary mother bore a striking resemblance to Harriet Nelson of the series "Here Come the Nelsons," and my dream dad was, of course, just like Ozzie Nelson. I made up brothers and sisters and we all went out for dinner and on vacations and generally lived a very happy life… in my mind. My problem was the feeling of dread, that sometimes bordered on panic, that my friends would come into contact with my real family. It was for that reason that I didn't encourage Dad to go get Mom very often: What if she came to school, or came walking up the street when I happened to be walking with my friends? The whole idea of that possibility was so humiliating that my face would grow hot at the thought of it. I wasn't as worried about Dad running into me and my friends. If he was out, then he would be at one of the four beer joints in town so that was easy. On Sunday through Wednesday, anyone who wanted to be noticed by Dad would have to go stand in front of the T.V. screen. I didn't need to worry about him.

Mother did get home sometimes, but she didn't argue with Dad much anymore when he came home drunk. One time she talked him into taking her with him when he went out. They were both out late that night and when they got back, Mother was drunk and sick. She threw up that night and again a few times over the next two days. Elsmarie and I were disgusted with both of them. "How could you get so drunk?" my sister asked with her voice raised.

Mother was lying on the couch, looking sick and ashamed. "I shouldn't have done it," she said weakly.

"You and I ought to go get drunk, Eileen," Elsmarie said, looking at me with her eyebrows raised. "Let's make this a family thing. I know… let's all go out and get drunk together tonight."

"How you talk, Elsmarie," Mother said, "I could never have talked to my mother the way you talk to me."

"Your mother probably didn't go out and get drunk and then come home and throw up all night, either!"

"Well, she probably did, but I couldn't talk back no matter what they did," she said. "They both drank when they wanted to, but that wasn't up to me." Mom didn't usually sound mad anymore when she talked to any of us, but she sure was getting mad at Elsmarie.

"Well, nothing is up to me either, Mother, because if it was, we wouldn't be living in this dump right now." Elsmarie always had the. last word.

I thought Elsmarie was too bossy to everyone and I got tired of listening to her, but she made Dad listen sometimes about buying food and things and one night, she saved our lives. It was lucky she was home that night. We had both gotten tired of listening to Dad's drunken stories and had gone to bed, leaving him sitting at the kitchen table by himself. Sometime in the middle of the night, Elsmarie yelled, "Eileen! Get up!"

I opened my eyes and realized that I could hardly breathe; there was thick smoke coming from somewhere in the house. I jumped up and ran for the stairs and got to the bottom just about the same time as Elsmarie. Through the thick haze of smoke, we could see an eerie orange glow over on the couch right by Dad's head. "Daddy!" Elsmarie screamed. "Get up! The couch is on fire!" She got the front door open and I went over by the couch.

"Wake up, Daddy!" I yelled. "Get up so we can get the cushion outside. Come on! You're laying on a cushion that's about to go up in flames!" The smoke was rolling out the front door and the air was getting a little clearer in the house.

"Whats'a matter? What's all the yelling about?" Dad coughed, mumbled and tried to open his eyes, and grinned. "Hey what's my girl yelling about?" Then he put his head back down.

"Shit!" Elsmarie said, "You hold his head up, Eileen, and I'll get the cushion and get it outside before it bursts into flames."

"Well, be careful!" I said. I did what she said. I held up Dad's

69

head and Elsmarie grabbed the cushion by a corner and ran out the door with it. I stood there holding up Dad's head and, not knowing what else to do, I just laid it gently down as he snorted in a big gulp of air, coughed, sighed and started snoring. I went out and joined Elsmarie on the front lawn where she stood by the smoldering cushion. The smoke rolled up into the air like a funnel. I looked up and down the road and didn't see a soul. "I hope no one called the fire department," I said.

"No, I don't think anyone is up." she said. "Shit! We could have all been burned up in there! Shit!" I'd seen her really mad before, but never this bad. "He's still sleeping, isn't he? Well, he's not going to be sleeping long!" She marched back into the house and kept after Dad until he woke up. I followed right behind her. "Dad! You wake up and see what you did! We could have all been killed!"

"Huh?" Dad was fumbling for a pillow for under his head. "Hey, who took my pillow?" he mumbled.

"Forget it!" Elsmarie said, "Let's take our blankets out on the porch and sleep out there."

It was easier for me to stick up for myself when Elsmarie was around. As long as I didn't try to cross her. If I got sick of hearing her play her record by Johnny Ray, called "Cry," then it was best if I kept it to myself because if I turned it off, it wouldn't matter what she was doing because in less than a minute after it stopped, she would come charging at you. "Did I say to turn that off?" she would scream. "You turn that back on, and start it at the beginning!"

Most of the time Elsmarie was gone. She was either at her girlfriends' house, or at the skating rink, or out with Rodney. I was never out late so usually it was just Dad and me in that house on the Boulevard. I was the one who was home, so I had to listen to him when he was drunk. One of Dad's favorite stories was how he took his first drink. This was always repeated somewhere between the hours of midnight and three A.M. after he had come stumbling in from the bar up the street. I would be called to the table to hear why he had gotten drunk that night. "Eileen!" His words would be slow and slurred, "Eileen! Come on down here and sit with your old man." Then he might sing one of his favorite songs.

On Monday we had bread and gravy,
On Tuesday was gravy and bread.
Wednesday and Thursday was gravy and toast,
But that's only gravy and bread.
So I said to my landlord on Friday,
Can you please give me something instead,
So on Saturday Morn, by the way of a change,
We had gravy without any bread.

"Pull up a chair and take a load off, kid. Do you know who gave me my first drink?" His face would be distorted into a grimace like he was really concentrating on getting his words out and he looked so different from the person that sat quietly in the chair staring at the snowy images on the old black and white T.V. in the living room when he was broke.

"My brother, Efram, that's who." The six-pack he brought home would be partially pulled from a brown paper bag on the table and his arm would sway out of range with his mouth a few times before he could successfully get the dark brown bottle to his lips. "You know I used to play in the drum and bugle core of the Salvation Army, and when we went out of town, guess what Efram would do? He'd drink and when I was just a kid he gave me my first drink."

I was glad he had gotten home, but after a while I'd get tired and want to get it over with so I could go to bed, especially on school nights. If there was spit in the corners of his mouth, he usually didn't last long before he'd stagger over to the couch and pass out. It was my job then to take the lit cigarette out of his hand and snub it out in the ashtray before I went back to bed. If there was no spit in the corners of his mouth it could be a long night of listening. The stories were always the same. I knew them by heart. How hard it was for him raising two daughters while Irene was off in the nut house. And if he got into the Irene stories he usually went all the way back to how jealous she was of the nurse in the hospital when he got hurt in the fire. That was before I was even born.

"They treated me like a king!" he would say. "And the red-headed nurse was extra good to me. Every now and then, she'd slip me a beer when she started her shift. You should have seen Irene

71

come running in the room, expecting to find me doing something, and me flat on my back with a broken ankle and a broken back. That's how she was."

When Dad got hurt in the fire, it made him something like a hero. There was a huge fire downtown and a brick wall or something fell on him and he was hurt real bad. He was hurt bad enough that they offered him his pension, but he turned it down. He probably should have taken it because he always had trouble with his ankle after that. He never really complained, but he always limped at the end of a day's work right up until he retired. Dad worked as a city fireman for seventeen years and then, all of a sudden, he didn't anymore. So he got a job down by Brooklyn Square in a plating factory and I guess those are the only two jobs he had his whole life. I think he used to miss some work when he was a fireman, but I don't think he ever missed at the plating works. He usually went out on Thursday nights after he got paid, but somehow he'd get himself straightened up by Friday morning in time to go to work.

I didn't mind the fireman stories. I didn't like the one about when Carol died. "Do you know we were married five years before that kid was born? I was beginning to think that Irene couldn't have any kids when she finally got pregnant with Carol. Irene must have been crazy way back when Carol died. I came home from work and there that poor baby was propped up in the high chair… she could hardly hold her head up and Irene was trying to make her eat." There would be a long silence and then he would say, "You know, the doctor stayed all night long, but he couldn't do anything to save her. That meningitis is bad stuff. Takes 'em quick. Right after she got baptized, too… I said I'd never have another kid baptized again."

That story made him sad, and me, too. Thankfully, he only told it when he was really blasted and his face, already transformed by the drink, would twist even more as he recalled his first child dead at nine months old. It wouldn't be long before he was passed out. I had learned from the couch fire that I had to stay up until he finally lay down and was out for the night so I could get the lit cigarette out of his hand.

Over those years, during Dad's late-night drunken ramblings, I learned the family history. Dad was born in Jamestown, New York, in 1909. The family immigrated from Jonkoping, Sweden in 1903 and are officially registered on the American Immigrant Wall of Honor at Ellis Island. The trials of that journey are recorded in a diary kept by my grandmother. The family was deeply involved in the Swedish Salvation Army Temple. Dad was the baby, born to his mother after her 46th birthday. He had nieces and nephews who were older than he. He had four sisters and one brother. The brother was the second oldest child in his family and much older than Dad. My father came into his family during a time of prosperity for his parents and he was used to having things his own way.

My mother and her family, unlike Dad's family, were not solid middle-class, and they were not cornerstones of the Salvation Army Temple. Mother was the second oldest of four children and the first daughter in her family. She was nearly twenty when her baby brother was born and it was up to her to help take care of the younger children in the family. Mother and Dad met while she was attending services at the Army. Mother fell for Dad right away. He was tall, slim and had deep blue eyes and thick light-colored hair that lay in waves on top of his head. Mother was almost a head shorter than Daddy with dark brown hair and pretty brown eyes. Their looks complemented each other in all of the photographs of them. They soon became childhood sweethearts. When Dad was drunk, he would say, "I wasn't sure that I wanted to marry Irene at all, but my mother said that we had gone together so long that she and her family would expect it, so what could I do?"

I didn't like hearing the stories over and over, and I felt funny listening to him say mean things about Mother all the time, and he would make fun of the things she did, he laughed at her recipe collection and he would call her Sweetie Face in a sneering way. Sometimes I wanted to tell him that I didn't like it, but I was afraid of making him mad at me. I just wished that we could live like other people.

Everyone I knew had a pretty house, and when my friends invited me in, their mothers were always home. One day, I was at Nancy's house and I watched her mother fold laundry and put the clothes on the dining room table for each person in the family. There was a whole pile of panties that belonged just to Nancy. I couldn't get over that. Sometimes, on the weekends, I would be invited to stay overnight and then I would pretend to call home for permission. Usually, I would say, "My mother said I can't stay over because we have company coming."

I would have loved to stay over with them, but then who would take the lit cigarette out of Dad's hand when he passed out so the house wouldn't burn down?

I couldn't figure out why Nancy's family worked so well and mine didn't. It seemed like all of our relatives were also doing better than we were; what could be making the difference? I wanted to believe in God and I got down on my knees in the dark bedroom upstairs many, many nights. "Please, God! Please, please let my mother come home and make my dad stop drinking. I'll be good. I'll do anything you want me to, but please help my family." I knew that other people prayed in church and my aunts seemed to pray all the time and it worked for them. Dad said that no one else could get through to God, because He was always having to listen to Aunt Mildred.

Most of it seemed kind of unbelievable. For instance, it seemed to me that if we were supposed to love God, then He should love us back and He shouldn't pick out just certain people to love and not others. I might not have believed anything about God at all except for that one time when I was at the Salvation Army and my cousin, Ritchie, went up to the alter. He was a big boy, then...probably about twelve and he went up to give his heart to Jesus. He cried very hard up there and the person who was helping him said he was just cleansing his heart and soul for Jesus. I just knew that something special had happened to Ritchie. It made me believe.

There was something I wasn't doing right and that's why my prayers were not being answered. One time I asked Dad, "How come we don't go to the Salvation Army like your sisters and their families? Maybe things would work out better for us if we did. We wouldn't have to sit with Aunt Mildred. We could sit with Farmor and Aunt Anna."

"Okay, now you sound just like your Aunt Mildred! That's all I've ever heard all my life from them. Go to the church! Pray to God!" His voice sounded really mad. "Well, praying never got me anything. I tried that and what'd it get me? A crazy wife and a dead baby. Do you think it's easy for me trying to raise you girls all by myself? Do you think I don't know what your sister is doing in that house up there with her boyfriend?" He kind of laughed a drunk nasty laugh. "I know what they're doing. I suppose you're doing it too, with some boy. Let me ask you something, are you a virgin?"

"No, Daddy, honest I'm not!" I didn't know what a virgin was, but it must be bad, as mad as he sounded.

"Oh. Well, that's just swell!" He leaned back in his chair and as he did some of his beer spilled onto the front of his shirt, but he didn't seem to notice. "Well, I'm sorry I asked."

"Well, am I supposed to be one?" I was confused now because he didn't seem to like my answer. "If I'm supposed to be one, then I guess I am if it has something to do with a boy."

"Okay," he said, "You're still my little sweetheart, aren't you? Well, don't you ever do nothing like your sister's doing."

One day I came home and Elsmarie and her boyfriend, Rodney, and Dad were all sitting in the living room. I just knew something bad had happened because she was crying and Dad looked very serious. "What's wrong?" I asked. "I hope no one died."

"Your sister is getting married next week." Dad sounded mad. The room was so quiet after he said that, the only thing you could hear was a big black fly buzzing around the front window. Rodney was sitting as close as he could get to Elsmarie and he had his arm tightly around her shoulders. He looked good when he was all cleaned up to come for her and take her on a date. He usually wore bright-colored sweaters with V-necks and dressy shirts underneath. He had broad shoulders and he was tall, but not as tall as Daddy. He wore thick glasses, but he had nice, friendly eyes, although now they were very serious and instead of being dressed up, he was wearing work clothes.

"So you won't live here anymore, will you?" My own voice didn't sound right. I thought about how stupid that sounded. Of course she wouldn't live with us anymore.

Elsmarie lifted a tear-streaked face up towards me. "I'll just be up the street. Rodney's mother and father are fixing up a little apartment for us upstairs in their house. You can come and see me any time you want to. Okay? Will you come and see me?"

She looked different lately since she had been going with Rodney. She looked better. She said that Rodney's mother had taken her shopping for some new clothes and had taken her downtown to get her hair fixed. I always thought she looked better than me, anyway. She was skinny, but not as skinny as me. Most of all I hated being skinny. Rodney's mother bought a dress for me to wear to the wedding. It was made of a shiny light brown material and it had silver leaves on it. I thought it was very pretty.

That morning before the wedding, Elsmarie tried to fix my hair. She just seemed to cry all the time since they decided to get married, "You be sure to come up and see me, okay?" she said in between snuffing the stuff up her nose before it dripped down onto her chin. "I'm going to be there for you, no matter what. Okay?"

I tried to nod and she said, "Hold still, or I can't fix your hair!"

"Aren't you going to have Ma at your wedding?" I asked. "She should come, too." I added softly, hoping not to make her mad by saying that.

"I know she should be there, but there isn't time to go get her. You know Rodney's mother and dad are paying for everything and they want to have it right now, so I'm going along with it. Rodney and I are going to go see her next Sunday and tell her all about it so she won't feel bad."

Six months after Elsmarie and Rodney's wedding, we had to go back to the little chapel downtown where they got married. This time we had to go to a funeral for Elsmarie's little baby. Deborah was born with something wrong with her lungs and she couldn't live. Poor Elsmarie was still in the hospital and couldn't even go to the funeral. I had to go, but I hated seeing that poor little baby that way. Rodney kept crying all through the service and before the man closed the tiny white casket, Rodney just kept holding little Deborah's hand. It was awful. I was just glad that no one took any pictures of the little baby in the casket.

I didn't understand what I was doing wrong because God didn't listen to any of my prayers. I had prayed for that little baby when I heard there was something wrong with her lungs. And then God went on and made her die anyway. Maybe Aunt Mildred was right.

You can't go to Heaven if you don't go to Church. The Celoron Methodist Church was about to get a new member.

VIII

The Celoron Methodist Church was just four blocks away from the Boulevard. It was only about half the size of the Swedish Salvation Army Temple where Dad's family went. There was a short stairway that led up to big double doors, and when you went in, you were in a small entrance way where papers and pamphlets were kept on a table. The stairway to the basement was right there too. Downstairs was the fellowship hall and that's where most of the Sunday School classes were held. Upstairs was where the Church service was held. It looked nice. There were shiny wooden pews to sit on and blue carpeting on the floor. In the front was an alter with plenty of kneeling space and there was room for the organ and the place where the minister preached his sermons. There were also chairs for the minister and the choir to sit on behind the altar.

Mainly, I hoped that going would save my family. It was a fact that Dad's sisters and their families spent most of their time in church and God was so interested in helping them that He even made sure that their bread recipes turned out fine. Maybe if I showed up every Sunday He would send a few Blessings our way. Maybe Dad would stop drinking and Mother would be able to get out of the hospital and we could just have our little family together. But I said an extra little prayer as I was going in the door for the very first time. "Please God, don't let me act mean like Aunt Mildred." That must have been on Dad's mind, too, after I started going, because he said almost the same thing.

"Jesus Christ, I hope she doesn't turn out like Mildred," I heard him say to Elsmarie one day after I invited both of them to go with me to Church.

Reverend Cooke was really happy to see me in church. I met him after the service that first Sunday. There I was, lined up with everyone else to go out the door and next thing I knew I was face to face with him. He took my one hand in both of his. His hands were warm, but not sweaty. I was afraid mine was sweaty. "Welcome! It's so good to see you here!" He had a very nice face. It was a thin face with a sharp little nose and chin, but he had a really good smile and his eyes were very friendly. "What is your name?" he asked in a big voice.

"It's Eileen," I answered in a small voice.

"What a beautiful name! Are your folks here?" He raised his eyebrows and looked around as he asked and then looked back at me.

"No," I said, and I told him about my mother working nights at the hospital and having to sleep during the day.

"Well, I'm glad you don't work nights and you can come." H⟨ showed me that big smile again and gave my hand an extra squ⟨ before he let go and then he started talking to someone behi⟨

I couldn't stop thinking about how my family could ch⟨ that I was going to church. And I went back the next week, ⟨ week after that. Nothing new was happening at home yet, but ⟨ as I lay in my bed at night, I could see how everything wou⟨ happen. I could see myself coming home from church one day and both of my parents would be there. I would walk in the door and see the house clean and the table would be set for five people. Elsmarie and Rodney would be sitting together in the living room and they would smile at me when I came in. There would be a good meal on the table in serving dishes and my mother and father would walk into the dining room from the kitchen carrying a cake. "She's home!" Dad would say.

Mother would be wearing a pretty dress and her hair would be curled and when she smiled she would have teeth where the empty spaces were. "We're so glad you're home," she would say, "and we've arranged a celebration dinner in your honor because if it wasn't for your prayers and your Faith in God, I wouldn't be home for good from the hospital."

"And I wouldn't have quit drinking," Dad would say, "We're going to have a happy family and we owe it all to you."

I knew I probably had to be patient, because Reverend Cooke said that God works in His own time. I knew my plan could take a few months, so I just decided that it would give me a chance to do more

at the church. The very next Sunday, Reverend Cooke said, "We could use another voice in the choir, Eileen, and don't forget Confirmation Classes start next Saturday."

That was it! That would be the day that my family would come together. Mother told me that she was confirmed and she even said that Elsmarie and I should take Confirmation at a church sometime. She said that Dad was confirmed, too. I was excited because I could see how my plan was going to work. Reverend Cooke had told us that we had to get our parents to sign a paper giving their permission for us to be confirmed, and he said, "This is a very solemn and important step for you and your parents. They will want to know the date of your Confirmation, because they will definitely want to attend."

I practically ran home with my paper in my hand that Sunday after Church so I could have Dad sign it. He was sitting at the table, looking like he always did on Sunday, like he was sorry for everything he'd one all weekend. "Daddy, look, I'm going to get confirmed. Will you sign my permission paper? Reverend Cooke said we all have to get our parents to sign." I unfolded it and laid it in front of him and then went to find a pen for him in my school bag.

"Sure I will, Honey. I'll sign your paper. So you're going to be confirmed, are you? Well, I think that's wonderful. Let me see where I sign… I hope I'm steady enough."

"You're going to come, aren't you, Daddy? It's going to be on Palm Sunday… you know, that's the week before Easter."

"I know I'm no good when I'm drinking, but I still know when Palm Sunday is. Sure I'll be there, Honey." He sounded almost like he wanted to cry. He cried when he was drunk, but I'd only seen him cry once when he was sober and that was when his mother died four years ago. "And I'm not going to drink anymore either from now on."

"Dad, will you get Mother home for my Confirmation? She should be there." I was hoping that my asking wouldn't hurt his feelings.

"Sure, I'll go down and get her. Don't worry, she'll be there," he said. I was sure that I saw him look like he was thinking hard about everything all that day right up until the "Ed Sullivan Show" came on television. I felt like the plan was already in action. I didn't tell Elsmarie about it because I figured she'd never believe it. I did ask her, though, if she had some idea where we could get a nice dress for Mother. "Just in case she's home the day I get confirmed, she needs something decent to wear," I said, trying to sound like it didn't really matter.

"I don't know, maybe Rodney's mother would have some ideas. Mother could use some clothes anyhow. I'll talk to her." Elsmarie acted like she was always glad to see me when I would visit her in her apartment. The stairway was in the back of the house and it was enclosed all the way up, but it was separate from Rodney's parents' house. The apartment was small, but it was really nice. The hardwood floors were shiny and she had some pretty scatter rugs down in some places. She had nice furniture and there were some pretty things sitting around on the tables and pictures on the walls. Elsmarie kept it really clean and it smelled nice in there. She was sad for a long time after her baby, Deborah, died. She told me she could hear that baby crying in the middle of the night. I didn't know what to say to her so I never stayed very long.

The next few weeks went fast. I went to church on Wednesday nights for choir practice and Saturday mornings for Confirmation classes and, of course, on Sunday mornings for church. Dad kept getting drunk, but I felt like it wouldn't be for much longer because I just knew that our family would get Blessed on Palm Sunday. During the time that I wasn't in church I was babysitting. It wasn't a very good job because I was taking care of Edna Drake's son's kids. Edna Drake is the lady who owned Glamour Manor; her house was nasty and her son's house was nasty, too. There were six kids, but the youngest was three, so I didn't have to take care of any babies.

Jimmy Drake and his wife, Gloria, bought a huge old house on Conewango Street. It was one of those houses that used to be a mansion for some rich people and had about fourteen rooms and that was the only good part of the babysitting job. With that many rooms those six kids could chase each other around and scream at each other all they wanted, but you didn't have to hear all of it. The rooms on the third floor didn't have any furniture in them and they liked playing up there and the way they yelled I just hoped they wouldn't kill each other. The biggest kid was only about two years younger than me, so there wasn't much I could do to stop him from doing anything he wanted to do. The worst thing about the job is when all the kids decided to sit in the living room and be quiet for a television program because every one of them would sit and pick their noses and wipe it on the furniture. It was hard to find a place to sit where there wasn't dried slimy stuff and it made me sick to my stomach, but the Drakes paid good and came home when they were supposed to. I made enough money to buy myself a new dress and shoes for Confirmation.

Mrs. Anderson was a big woman, but not fat. She was tall and solid looking with reddish brown hair that was very curly even though it was neatly tied back. She treated everyone the same and expected the very best from us. She was the choir director, and not only did she make new choir robes for us, but she was teaching us some very special music to sing Easter Sunday. She was choosing people to do short little solo parts and she wanted me to do one of the parts. "I can't do it, Mrs. Anderson," I said. "I could never sing by myself in front of other people." Just the thought of it made my mouth get dry.

"Sure you can... you've got a fine alto voice and this part is for an alto. Come on... give it a try." She had a way about her to make people want to do things.

"Okay," I said weakly, "I'll try." It was two lines, that's all, and I was going to do it. The next week we found out that our choir had been invited to sing with several other choirs at the Epworth Methodist Church in Jamestown for a special service on Easter Sunday evening. I was going to have to sing my solo there in front of everyone at that big church. I was scared. All of a sudden, there were so many things happening all at once that I didn't know how I could get through everything. I thought about going to talk to Reverend Cooke in private, but he was busy all the time. He' walk through the church when we were having choir practice and stop for a minute and listen to us sing, and then he'd give us a big grin and the thumbs up sign and off he'd go. Someone said he visited the hospitals downtown during the week and people in Celoron who were too old or sick to come to church. I liked him so much. I decided when I grew up I would marry a minister just like him and I hoped his wife knew how lucky she was. She was kind of thin, just like him, and she would come on Sundays and sit in the first pew with their three little girls.

Confirmation Day was finally just one week away. I started reminding Dad on the Sunday before so he'd have the whole week to plan. "Don't forget, Daddy. You've got to get Mother and you have to come to my Confirmation next Sunday," I told him.

"Okay. Okay, don't worry about it. We'll all be there," he said.

Usually I didn't say anything to him on Monday or Tuesday to remind him of his promise not to get drunk on Thursday because he got mad when I said too much. Even when I reminded him on Wednesday, he didn't like it. "Now don't start nagging about that, Eileen. I already told you I'm coming right home after work on payday. Now don't wear it out!"

I learned not to nag him too much because it could have the reverse effect. A few times he got drunk because he said that's all I did was nag him about drinking and he couldn't take it anymore. I had to be very careful so the plan of everyone coming together as a family would work out. Every time Reverend Cooke told us to have a little silent prayer to ask God for what we needed, I prayed for our family. I believed I was doing everything good now, so God shouldn't be mad at me anymore for not thinking about church very much. I had also been nicer about writing letters to Mother, and I cleaned up the house every day after school. I even baked a chocolate pudding pie one day for the lonely old man that always walked by himself all over town and took it to where he lived. That might have been a mistake because he kept trying to talk me into coming over and sitting on his lap and I had a real funny feeling about what he might do so I just said, "I hope you like your pie. I've got to go now," and left right away. I didn't tell Elsmarie about that when I stopped to remind her about Sunday. She would have said that was really a stupid thing to do, and I guess I already found that out.

Thursday came and Daddy didn't come home. School was out for Spring vacation, so I waited up for him even though it was after two

83

o'clock in the morning when he finally made it. He was blasted. He looked as bad as I'd ever seen him. "Daddy!" I just yelled at him, "You promised me you'd come right home. You can't spend all your money now! You've got to go get Mother on Saturday so you can both come to my Confirmation on Sunday. You promised!"

He had a hard time focusing his eyes on me because his head kept weaving back and forth from the place on the couch where he had plopped himself. "Look here. Now I was just going to stop and have a couple so I could cash my check and I ran into my old friend Skoogie."

"Daddy, you promised you'd go get Mother on Saturday for my Confirmation!" I didn't want to hear his old stories.

"Listen, Eileen. I hope you aren't turning into one of those religious fanatics, are you?" He was having trouble getting his words to come out. "I'm serious. I'm worried about you. Jesus Christ, you're hanging out at that church every time I turn around. I don't even see you anymore. Every night of the week and on Sundays, too. That can't be healthy."

"I'm not there every night of the week. I'm babysitting every night except Wednesday. I told you that. So you're not coming." I didn't want to talk to him anymore.

"I'll be there. I'll be there. I didn't say I wasn't coming. This was just for tonight. I'll be home tomorrow night and I'll go get Irene on Saturday. Don't get excited," he said, the last word kind of trailing off so you couldn't hear all of it, and then his head dropped down on his chest and he was snoring.

I guess he managed to get himself to work on Friday morning because I didn't see him at all that evening. I went to bed about twelve thirty and hoped that he wouldn't burn the house down after he got home. I had to get up early for my last Confirmation class. He wasn't home again when I got up in the morning, if he even came home. I still hung on to a little bit of hope that Dad was going to go get Mother so she would be able to come to church on Sunday. If you believed in God, then you had to believe in miracles.

At Confirmation class we practiced how we would sit and what we should do when we were called up front. Reverend Cooke said that the first three rows would be reserved for our families and there would be white bows at the ends of each of the three rows so people who weren't in our immediate families wouldn't sit there. He told us to explain to our parents about the seating so they wouldn't have to move forward once they were seated. After class I waited for the other kids to leave and then I said, "Reverend Cooke, my family might not be able to come tomorrow, so I might not be here."

"Eileen," he came over to me and said in the most gentle voice I'd ever heard coming from a man, "if your family can't come, then you have an added responsibility to come for them. Do you understand? We must all come and be confirmed for ourselves, but also for those who, for whatever reason, can't do it themselves." He placed his hand on my shoulder gently.

I said, "I'll be here and be confirmed. Thank you." I went running out of the church because I was afraid I'd cry.

After class that day, I felt all calm inside. I didn't think about Daddy anymore, but I felt sad for Mother because I had written her and told her she was going to come home and see me confirmed, but I knew I couldn't help it and I would write her another letter and tell her about it after it was over. The next morning, I got up early and put on my new dress and shoes. I had washed my hair and put it up in curlers the night before and it was shiny and curly for church. When I went downstairs, Daddy was sitting at the table looking sad the way he always did on Sundays, but I didn't have time to stop and talk with him. "See you later, Dad," I said as I walked out the door.

The service at the church was beautiful. I was baptized for the first time and was able to answer my Confirmation question at the altar that Reverend Cooke asked, and with his usual big smile he confirmed me. After church, all the other parents came up and congratulated me just like they did with all the other kids. Mrs. Anderson said, "Don't make any plans for next Saturday morning, we need to have choir practice Wednesday and Saturday so we can be ready for the service downtown on Sunday Evening. By the way, you all look great!"

Finally everyone was going out the door and filing past Reverend Cooke. He said to me, "We're going to have a surprise before we practice on Wednesday. A special youth minister is going to be here and give a little service. He's great! See you then."

I felt so good coming home from church that I just wanted to tell someone. I stopped at Elsmarie's apartment. I knocked and didn't hear anything from inside and I was just heading back to the stairs when Rodney opened the door. He looked all rumpled from sleep. "Hi. Come on in, your sister's in the living room."

I walked through to the living room and saw Elsmarie lying on the couch with a washcloth on her head. Her eyes looked like they were still half asleep and her hair was all mashed on one side of her head. "What's wrong, Elsmarie? I asked.

She opened her eyes and looked at me and said, "Oh God! I missed your Confirmation, didn't I? I'm sorry. We went out last night and–"

"It's okay," I interrupted her, "but I wish you could have seen it. It was so nice and everyone treated me very nice." I realized that I had a good day, and my family didn't.

She had closed her eyes again. She opened them like little slits and asked, "Did Dad go?"

"No, but–" I started to say it was all right when she cut me off.

"It figures," she said. And she moaned and said, "Oh Eileen, You're so damn good and I'm so damn hung over. I'm really sorry."

"It's okay," I said again, "Don't worry about it. I'm going to go so you can start to feel better. Maybe I'll see you later."

The youth minister that Reverend Cooke told me about on Sunday did come on Wednesday night. He said that we should call him Joe. We had a service with him before we started our choir practice. No one could figure out at first why he was wearing dark glasses inside the church and then he told us that he was blind. Joe had a wonderful way of talking about God and the way that He had blessed him. He said that when we are missing something that we really need and wish we had, then God will give us other things to take the place of those things that we don't have. He said God blessed him with the will and the words to talk to young people and He also blessed him with a singing ability. Then he sang with the most beautiful tenor voice I had ever heard. At the end of his service he called us to come forward and give our hearts to Jesus.

I had been called before and I had tried to will myself to go forward because I believed it was the right thing to do, but always before, I just couldn't make myself get up. That night was different. Joe would sing a little, and then he'd urge us to come, and then he'd sing some more. I felt a need to go forward. It was like being hungry and being called to supper and before I could even think about it, my feet were carrying me up to that altar. I finally understood what my cousin, Ritchie, must have felt all those years ago at the Salvation Army and why he was crying so hard the night he gave his heart to the Lord. I knew it because I was crying just as hard and I didn't feel any shame about it. It was a wonderful feeling of letting go, followed by a deep sense of peace.

Two other girls went up to be saved that night, too. All three of us hugged each other after, and Reverend Cooke hugged all of us. When I got to shake Joe's hand after the service I realized that I had his one hand in both of mine just the way Reverend Cooke did with everyone and I wasn't even planning it. It made me feel proud and happy. Like maybe I was getting really nice, too.

Our choir practice was the best it had ever been, including my solo. I sang it right out at church on Easter Sunday and at the Epworth Methodist Church that night... I wasn't nervous, even though the church was so packed that people were standing all the way out to the front stairs. I did very well and I knew that it was God that helped me get through it. It was a wonderful time for me and I wanted the good feeling to go on forever, but of course, it couldn't.

The things I wanted to change always stayed the same, and the things I didn't want to change almost always did. Not long after Easter, Reverend Cooke announced, tearfully, that he would be leaving the Celoron Methodist Church. He said he had been asked to take another church somewhere in Pennsylvania and that a Reverend McEntarfer would be coming to take his place and he wanted us to give our loyalty to him.

I tried to give the new minister the same loyalty that I felt towards Reverend Cooke, but it was very hard because they were so different. Reverend McEntarfer was nice enough and I think he was sincere, but he was an older man and he just acted tired all the time. I kept on going on Sundays for a while, but then I started skipping now and then and finally I just stopped going. I was doing so much babysitting on Saturday nights that it was hard for me to get up

Sunday mornings.

I was buying more clothes and figured out that I should only wear some clothes once and then wash them before I wore them again. I was taking a bath every day and I started taking better care of my hair. The other kids were getting to be more friendly and I spent a lot of time lately thinking about a boy in my class.

Rodney and Elsmarie started going down to get Mother. The first time she came home after my Confirmation I told her all about it and she said, "I wish I could have been there." She wanted to know everything about it. She asked how many kids were confirmed and if there were flowers on the altar and what the other girls' dresses were like. She even asked what Confirmation question Reverend Cooke asked me. She told me some things about her Confirmation Day and, realizing just how much it meant to her, I began to feel horrible about the fact that she had missed mine.

It was times like that when I really felt bad that she wasn't home. She seemed to always be so interested in everything about me. "You should have been there, but you know how Dad is. He can't stay sober for anything." I was more hurt for her than for myself at this point.

"Now, don't talk that way about your father," she said, "He works hard and he deserves a little fun."

"A little fun?" I repeated. I couldn't believe she would say that. "How can you stick up for him? He doesn't stick up for you! I think you should stay home and he ought to go to the hospital!"

"Now, no matter what he does, he's still your father and you shouldn't say those things about him!" She was getting very upset with me.

I just shook my head, "Okay, Mother. Okay. I won't say anything more about him. But I just want to say this: I think you should get out of that hospital and just stay home. Why can't you just come home?"

"I can't go home until someone signs me out." she said.

"Like who? Do you mean like a doctor?

"No," she said. "Someone like your father could do it. My mother could do it, but whoever does it has to sign a paper saying they are responsible for me, and your Grandpa Stewart doesn't want

Grandma to sign a paper like that, so she can't do it. He's the boss over her."

We were sitting at the table and we had just eaten the sandwiches that she made for us for lunch. Mother's eyes were warm and clear, but they started to water some when I asked, "So why doesn't Dad sign you out?"

"I guess he has his reasons," she said. "Someday he will." She reached in her dress pocket for some of her toilet paper and wiped her eyes and looked away from me.

"So until then... you just have to sit out there in that hospital and wait? I thought it was because the doctors didn't want to let you go, I didn't know it was Dad who was keeping you there."

"Well, maybe the doctors won't let me go, but they don't have to even decide that until someone wants to sign me out. And then I would have to go home for a thirty-day trial period and then go before the board. That's how they do it." She could see the expression of shock on my face. "It's not so bad at the hospital anymore. You know that I'm in Building A now and I get to come and go pretty much when I want to. We have dances sometimes on Saturday nights. I work at the laundry everyday and I earn a little money so I can have something to spend at the store. You know what I mean, the store at the hospital. I've taken you there. They sell ice cream and coffee, and magazines; some other little things that I like to buy once in a while. And I have a lot of friends at the hospital." She looked away and said, "Sure, I'd rather be home, but there's nothing I can do."

I wanted to go find Dad and scream at him. I wanted to grab him by his shirt and pull him off a barstool and throw him on the floor and get right in his face and say, "Do you mean my mother has been kept in a mental hospital all these years because you won't sign her out?" It was just coming together for me. I thought about all the times over the years that I'd had to listen to him while he rambled on in his drunken stupor that the reason he drank was because his wife was in the nuthouse and it was just too hard trying to raise two girls on his own. I was even supposed to feel grateful to him for doing the right thing. He said that she had been there so long that all he would have to do is sign a paper and he could be divorced and free of her once and for all. So many things to say all came together at once and I just sat there.

Mother got up from the table and started clearing the dishes away. "I'm going to take the bus downtown this afternoon," she said, "Do you want to go with me? I've saved up a few dollars and I'll buy you something."

"No, Mother, I have to do some homework this afternoon, but you go", I said "And let me give you some money. I've been saving my babysitting money and I want you to buy something for yourself." I started to go upstairs for my money.

"No," she said, "I don't want you giving me your money. You buy something for yourself. You need nice things for school. I don't need anything, anyway."

There didn't seem anything else to say. "I'm going to go read my schoolbook. I'll see you later." It wasn't actually a school book for homework, but it was a library book. I loved reading books and over the two years that we had been in Celoron I had read just about every book in the school library. That was just one reason I would be glad to leave sixth grade and go to junior high for seventh grade. It would be a new school and a new start.

IX

Sometimes I tried to imagine what it would have been like if Mother had been home all the time. Most of the time I thought it was probably best just the way things were because no one ever really bossed me around except Elsmarie when she was home. Daddy acted like he didn't care when I went to bed, or what I ate. I guess he just figured I was old enough to take care of myself. Some things might have been better, though. For instance, the way Mother always liked to iron clothes when she was home means the wrinkled dress thing never would have happened.

I had just started fifth grade and Mrs. Fredericks made each student come up to the chalkboard to work out a long division problem. I had just done mine and was heading back to my seat, when the teacher came up to me and said, "Eileen, why didn't your mother iron your dress?" She didn't say it right out loud, but it was loud enough so some people heard it in the front rows. I had never thought of it before, but I looked down at my dress and it was very wrinkled. I didn't know what to say, so I just went to my seat, but I never wore that dress again and I tried to iron my clothes after that. I was never as good at it as Mother was. She was excellent at ironing.

Mother probably wouldn't have been able to help with the birdhouse thing, but she would talked about it so much that Dad would have probably helped just to shut her up. Mrs. Fredericks loved birds and she talked about them a lot. One day she said someone else who loved birds had donated some money to our class so that each one of could have all the pieces of wood needed to build a birdhouse. Her husband came to school and showed us how we could put the pieces together with glue and little tiny nails. He even gave us the nails and said if we couldn't get the glue, then we could still put our birdhouses together with our little nails and then we could paint them ourselves. He said if we wanted to add to them we could, but we had to do the work on our own. We couldn't let our parents help us. Well, that was no problem for me; I was pretty sure my parents wouldn't help.

I did just what we were supposed to do with our birdhouses. I put it together and painted it all by myself. The pieces didn't go together very straight, so it was kind of crooked and the only paint I had was an old can of green left in the cubby hole under the stairs from the people who lived there before us. It was really hard to get the can open and inside the paint was thick and rubbery on top and thin and oily on the bottom. It didn't mix up very well, but I used it anyway. The day we were supposed to bring them to school we were told to line them up on the floor along the wall and the other teachers would come in at recess and judge them. The winner was to receive a prize.

My birdhouse didn't look anything like the other ones. There was one that was so big the boy's father had to bring it in. It was like a big apartment house for birds with six holes on each side. Another one was bright white with hand-painted flowers in soft pastel colors all around the front opening. There was another white one with red shutters attached at each side of the opening with a blue roof that made it look almost like the American flag. As you looked down the row of birdhouses you could see a rainbow of bright, glossy colors until you came to one almost at the end of the row. That one could have won the prize for the worst looking one of all with its dull green finish. It looked like it had been fished out of the lake and the wood had not matched up right on one side, causing it to lean a little to the left and there was a slight space between the house and the roof on that side. I knew that I would never build another birdhouse. Mrs. Fredericks was a good teacher, except for those things, and I liked her better than my fourth grade teacher at Celoron, Mrs. Haynes.

Mrs. Haynes was nosier than any teacher I ever had in school and I didn't even tell her any real bad lies the way I did my third grade teacher, Mrs. Allison at the Willard Street school. After that social worker came to the place on Tower Street wanting to know how many babies were in the house, I learned my lesson about stretching the truth too far.

Anyway, Mrs. Haynes was probably was trying to be nice, but I could never forgive her for what she did. She was the reason, more than anything else, that I hated that I had my appendix out at the beginning of fourth grade. Because of her that was the worst thing that happened that year. I made it to the doctor and through the operation after being dragged around to beer joints with Daddy all day, doubled up with pain in the back seat of his car. We thought it was just a stomach ache until someone at one of the bars where he stopped came out to see me while I was lying down in the back seat of the car and went in and told Dad to get me to the doctor. I had to lie in the hospital for ten days and listen to the mother of the little kid in the next bed talk babytalk to her six-year-old child all the while. Finally, Daddy came and got me and I went home, but I wasn't supposed to go back to school for two more weeks

I was fine and was enjoying the fact that I didn't have to worry about getting up early and dressing for school and I could lie around on the couch and watch "The Secret Storm" and "The Guiding Light" on television. That's just what I was doing when there was a knock on the door. My first thought was to jump up, run upstairs and hide, but I wasn't supposed to run up the stairs. Before I could even think it out clearly, the door opened and Mrs. Haynes poked her head in. "Eileen," she called, "it's Mrs. Haynes." And then she saw me, "There you are! My, I'm glad to see you. How are you, dear?" And she walked right in and sat down in the living room without even being invited.

I was so surprised and ashamed that I couldn't say anything. I couldn't believe it. Mrs. Haynes in her bright blue suit and white blouse that looked all silky and proper was sitting in Daddy's old chair. On the table next to her was a glass ashtray that was piled high with cigarette butts, and on the table by me was an old coffee cup and a bunch of toast crumbs. The afternoon sun was trying to shine through the dingy window and stained curtains and right on my old flannel pajamas that I'd had on since the day I came home from the hospital. I said, "Thank you for the present."

She had brought me a jigsaw puzzle in the shape of the United States. She acted like she didn't notice how horrible the house looked. "Now, Eileen, you have a long walk to school and part of it is uphill over that bridge. I don't think you should be walking that distance for the first few weeks, so I've arranged for you to ride the bus to school and back home."

"I thought the bus was only for kids in kindergarten," I said in a voice that didn't even sound like mine.

"Usually," she said, "but in cases like yours we make exceptions." She had stood up and put her hand on the doorknob, "Now you be sure to ride that bus, Eileen. You'll arrive at school earlier than the walkers so you come right to my room and I'll know that you're safe. You get well now and we'll see you when you get back." And she left.

I don't know which was worse: That I had been found out and now she knew how awful our house was; or that when I went back to school that next week I had to get up earlier than usual and run in order to make it over the bridge at the same time as the kindergarten bus. Did she really think I was going to ride the bus with all those little kids?

The other time she embarrassed me was when she stopped me on my way out after school one day and said, "Eileen, don't you eat lunch? You never buy a meal ticket so I thought you were bringing, but I've watched for two days now and you don't bring lunch either. Can't your father buy lunch for you?"

"Usually I bring lunch," I lied. "I just haven't been hungry these past two days. I'll bring it tomorrow." I didn't know just when the roaring noise started up again in my ears, but it was getting so loud I could hardly hear her voice.

"Well, I'm going to check and make sure you bring a lunch from now on because you need to eat something. If you don't bring it, then I'll talk to your dad about it," she said.

Now I'd have to figure some way to get her to stop thinking about it. The next morning I found some mayonnaise in the refrigerator and I made a sandwich with it and wrapped it up in waxed paper and stuck it in a bag to carry to school. I made sure Mrs. Haynes saw it as I walked in and I made sure I put it way in the back of the other lunches that were brought by the other kids in case she started snooping around to see what I brought. I really just wanted her to leave me alone. After a while I found a plastic sandwich container stuck back in one of our cupboards at the house. It was in the shape of a sandwich so on the days when we didn't have any bread to make a sandwich I just put that in the bag so it looked like I had a lunch and she didn't bother me about it anymore. Finishing sixth grade meant I could leave that school and I wouldn't have to see her anymore and I was very glad about that.

Sixth grade was my best year so far in school and it was because of my teacher, Mr. Brown. It probably helped that I had some better clothes from my babysitting money and I could take care of myself better than I ever could before. I guess while I was trying to be so good for my Confirmation at the church that I had also been very good at school because Mr. Brown announced that I had been chosen for the sixth grade girl Juvenile Decency Award given by the American Legion. Ralph Adams was chosen as the boy and it meant that we would have to go to a luncheon at the American Legion Hall to get our awards. Our parents were invited to come to the awards lunch, but I was used to not having mine come so it didn't bother me that no one came for me; besides, I got to ride with Mr. Brown and that made the other girls jealous because we were all in love with him. Too bad he was married.

I had always been skinny, but now I was very tall and skinny. My friend Nancy's mother said that we were all going through the awkward stage and we would all get through it. She didn't know that I had been awkward all my life, but there were other girls in my class at school who had suddenly grown tall and looked skinny, too. The other Nancy, Nancy Thompson, was even taller than me. It was good to have friends and be included in everything. We were learning things from each other about boys and sex. If somebody found out something new, then it would be whispered from one girl's ear to another until we all knew about it, except for Laura maybe. She had cerebral palsy and she wasn't like the rest of us, but I hoped she didn't feel bad because we didn't include her. I wanted to just start walking with her and sitting with her at lunch, but I couldn't take a chance on getting everyone mad at me so I just kept quiet. I did try to smile at her every chance I got so she would know that I liked her. If Mother knew about Laura she would have wanted to invite her to our house; that's the way she was.

95

It would have been nice to be able to invite my friends home for a pajama party. Susie Sampson's mother let her invite five friends for a pajama party. We had a good time making pizza from the mixes in the box and there was plenty of soda to drink. Her mother let us play records, and dance and practice cheerleading. I didn't know people could have so much fun. Nobody asked me about my mother anymore, or why I never invited people over to my house. They were good friends and it was times like that that I wished I dared to tell them all about my mother being in the hospital and my dad's drinking, but I just couldn't take the chance. What if I had to go back to what it was like when no one liked me? I couldn't go back to that.

There was more good news from Elsmarie. She was going to have another baby. They had waited two years because they felt that she had been too young at fifteen to have a baby so they decided to wait until she was seventeen. Margaret, who was called Peggy, was born healthy and beautiful. Everyone loved her. It was sad that Mother couldn't be home when she was born, but there wasn't time to get her and everyone had their minds focused on the baby. I was the one who called Mother at the hospital to tell her the news that she had another granddaughter.

As soon as I got the words out Mother started crying. It was hard for her to talk. "Is she healthy?"

"Sure she is! She's perfect and she's really pretty, Mother," I told her, hoping she would stop crying.

"I wanted to be there with Elsmarie."

"I know, Mother," I tried to explain gently, because I wished she could have been there, too. "It would have been better if you could have been here. I wish you were here now." I was afraid I might cry, too.

"Tell your Dad I want to come home," she said. After a long pause, during which I knew she was crying too hard to talk, she said, "Tell Elsmarie I'm happy about the baby and I'll be home as soon as I can."

I was starting to argue with Dad about Mother when he'd start telling his drunk stories. "Dad, I don't think you should talk that way about Mother to me," I told him one night when he was starting in again about how he could get a divorce just by signing a paper because she'd been there so long. "You wouldn't like it if I talked bad about your mother to you."

"Now wait a minute!" he got all huffy with me. "Don't you compare Irene with my mother!"

"Well, Irene is my mother! And I don't want to hear all those stories anymore. I've heard them hundreds of times!" Before I knew it, I was raising my voice to him.

"Well, what about me?" His voice reminded me of a kid whining. "I'm just the poor bastard who pays the bills around here. Do you think it's been easy on me raising two girls all by myself?"

"Then get her out of there, Dad! You won't have to do it alone anymore." I had to get up and leave the table when I started talking about Dad bringing Mother home because I felt really mad at him. I was almost afraid I would lose control. "Just get her out!" With that I'd leave the room and go upstairs, or out on the porch; anywhere to get away from him. I could hear him still talking to me even after I left the room, but I just didn't pay any attention to him.

Now that Elsmarie had a new baby to care for, she and Rodney would not be able to go down to get Mother as often as they did before. Dad didn't have a car and seeing as he was able to ride to work with a man who lived down the street, he probably wouldn't be getting one soon. I needed to figure out a way to get Mother home for Christmas and so she could see Peggy. Elsmarie was able to sign her out for a home visit. Maybe they'd let me sign her out next time and I could bring her home on the Greyhound Bus.

The next day, I visited Elsmarie and told her about wanting to go down on the bus and get Mother.

"It's real easy," she said, "I used to do it when I was about your age. I used to have Dad call and make the arrangements with her doctor's office and then tell them that I would be going in the building for her. They said it was fine as long as I was eighteen. I wasn't, but they never asked for proof."

"Did Dad call to make the arrangements when you and Rodney brought her home?"

"No, I didn't need him to call anymore. No, I just called and said I am her married daughter and I want to take her for a home visit. They always said that it was fine. I don't think they care, really. But, just in case, why don't I call and tell them I want to take her home and I'm sending you to get her because I have a new baby." Elsmarie was so happy since Peggy was born that she was always in a good mood. She looked me up and down and said, "You're what, thirteen now? You're certainly tall enough, but if I'm going to tell them you're eighteen, you better pile on some makeup and some extra clothes to cover up that little body."

It didn't take long for Elsmarie to make the arrangements. She only had to wait about two seconds for the person to check with Mother's doctor for permission before everything was set. I was about to make my first solo Greyhound trip.

X

I will always be grateful to the men and women who staffed the State Hospital at Helmuth and recognized that my mother was someone who was trustworthy, and tried to make her life bearable by giving her as much freedom as possible for a patient. There were several buildings contained within the tall iron fence that surrounded the facility, each building was lettered according to the severity of the condition of the patients. Mom was in Building A, where patients were not kept under lock and key. Most of the patients kept in that building worked somewhere on the grounds, either in one of the kitchens, the laundry, or as groundskeepers. They had the freedom to leave the building pretty much at will during the daytime hours and could shop on their own at the store. It was located right across the roadway from Building A. Patients were able to purchase personal grooming items, magazines, candy, small gifts, or get a bite to eat and a coffee at the small lunch counter in back. It was from the store that Mom would buy little gifts of hankies, or scarves to send to Elsmarie and me for our birthdays or Christmas when she couldn't get home.

My first trip to Helmuth on the Greyhound Bus seemed to take forever. Elsmarie would have made Rodney drive me in his car, but he was doing construction work down in Pennsylvania during the week. He had a long drive to get home on Friday nights and he had to leave early on Sunday in order to get back for Monday morning. I didn't mind. In fact, I felt good about it, because if this worked, then we wouldn't have to try to count on Dad anymore to see that Mother got home more often.

I decided to go on Saturday so we could all be together Sunday. Elsmarie was going to cook a dinner and invite Mother and Dad and me up so Mother could spend time with the baby. First, I had to ride the city bus the five miles from Celoron to Jamestown in order to hook up with the Greyhound Bus to Helmuth. I was able to get off right at the bus station, so that part was easy. I had to wait almost an hour before we left for Gowanda. I sat in the little coffee shop and ordered a coffee and a doughnut and hoped the people at the hospital would think I was eighteen when I got there to get Mother.

Gowanda was the name of the little town by the State Hospital at Helmuth. Lots of people just said that if you went crazy, you'd have to go to Gowanda. It usually took about an hour and a half by car to get to Gowanda from Jamestown, but it took more than two hours on the bus because they made stops in all the little towns along the way so people could get on or off. Once we got to Gowanda, I had to take a taxi the last few miles up the highway to the hospital. The driver was very nice when I asked him to take me right up to Building A and wait for me so I could get my mother. I told him we would be going right back down to Gowanda in just a minute. As we approached the building, my stomach got a little queasy and my mouth got dry. I was so nervous thinking that they wouldn't let me take her.

As soon as I got out of the car, she came up to me, "Look at you! Did you come all the way by yourself to get me?" She had been waiting on a park bench outside. Her face was pink from the cold even though the sun was shining. There was no telling how long she'd been there. "When they told me someone was coming this afternoon, I never dreamed it would be you. How can you be this grownup?" Her eyes were starting to water.

"Hi, Mother!" I gave her a little hug, "Don't cry, now. Listen; don't say anything about how old I am, or they won't let me sign you out. Okay? Just let me do the talking, Mom. Please?" I was walking towards the door as we talked.

"I won't say anything. I hope they let you do it." She looked worried, too. She followed behind me and we walked right in the building and rang the buzzer. Building A was the best building to be in if you had to be at Helmuth. People in there could leave the building whenever they wanted during the day. They had jobs on the hospital grounds and were free to walk wherever they wanted to within the gates of the place. Once you rang the buzzer in this building, the door automatically opened. There was a glass enclosed nurse's station just inside the door and I walked right up to it.

"I'm Irene Sandquist's daughter and I'm here to sign her out for a home visit." I tried to lower my voice and sound mature.

The nurse saw Mother behind me and said, "So this is your other daughter, Irene. She looks a lot like you. She looked me over pretty carefully and then smiled and put a paper in front of me, "Sign on the line that's marked for you. Oh, and put your date of birth on the line next to it." She smiled again and said, "Don't forget to include the year, 1939." She looked at Mother and said, "Have a nice time at home, Irene and bring back some pictures of your new granddaughter."

"I'll try to get a picture," she answered, and I saw tears again forming in her eyes again. She stood there smiling through tears wearing a bright blue cloth coat that was too big for her and she had a print scarf tied under her chin as a head covering. Her old black handbag bulged, probably with her recipes. "I'm glad you got to see my daughter, Eileen," she said.

I said, "Let's go, Mother," before she said something that would let the nurse know how young I really was. The December day was sunny but cold, and I noticed that Mother wasn't wearing gloves as we headed right out the door to the waiting taxi. I still couldn't believe that the nurse let us get away with it, but I wanted to get out of there before she changed her mind. "The nurse seemed really nice, Mom."

"Oh, she is! She's only been there for a couple of years, now. Most everyone here is nice to me. How long can I stay home?" she asked.

"You're home until after Christmas, as far as I know," I answered.

"Did your father call the doctor for me?"

She didn't say so, but I felt like she wanted it to have been Dad who called. I knew he didn't, but I didn't want to disappoint her so I just said, "Probably. I'm not sure, it was either him or Elsmarie. Wait until you see the baby!" I changed the subject.

"I can't wait!" But she didn't sound as excited as I thought she'd be. She used to be the one person in the family who got really excited about things. Whether it was Christmas or one of our

EILEEN SLOAN POWELL

birthdays or my Confirmation, she thought everything was special. If she was home, she'd make a big deal of it and if she had any money, she would make a cake, or a special supper. She'd always buy a present and wrap it up if she could. Sometimes, she could only wrap up a couple of hankies, and she would say, "It's just a little something. It's not much." But I always knew it was all she could afford.

I hated myself for being disappointed when I saw what was in her little packages. I knew somewhere inside of me that she was trying to make things right and that what she got was the best that she could afford, but I just wanted there to be something more in the package. It would have been easier if she had gotten mad at me for saying mean things to her like, "Ma, what'd you get this for? What am I supposed to do with this?" But she didn't get mad much anymore.

The ride back to Gowanda in the cab didn't take long. We got out at the place on Main Street where we had to wait for the bus. It was a combined drug store and lunch counter where they served coffee and sodas, or you could get a sandwich and a piece of pie. Mother had a cup of coffee and some peach pie. I really only like apple, pumpkin and lemon pie, but she liked all kinds of different things. "You should try some different foods," she said. "This is good pie and the coffee is good, too!"

I didn't think my cup of coffee was all that special. "It's just coffee, Ma, you make such a big deal about everything."

The bus came and we found a seat and settled in for the two-hour ride home. I didn't have much to say, but I tried to answer her questions. She wanted to know how Dad was and how I liked seventh grade and junior high school. "Are you still going to church?" she asked, "I should go with you while I'm home."

"No, I haven't been in a while. I've been babysitting on Saturday nights and the people don't get in until late so I'm really tired on Sunday mornings." I wondered if I should tell her that I started having my periods and that I woke up one morning and I was sure I had breast cancer because I was so sore in both of those places, but I didn't tell her. I told my friend Nancy, and she said her mother told her it was normal to hurt there because our breasts were just growing. I didn't tell my sister, and I sure didn't tell my dad. It would have seemed real strange to tell Mother anything like that. We didn't talk much for most of the trip back.

When we got back to Jamestown, it was late afternoon and the winter sun was already going down. It was cold. We had to walk two blocks down to Third and Main Streets to catch the bus home to Celoron. It wasn't coming until six o'clock so we would have to wait fifteen minutes. "Where's your gloves, Mother?" I asked. She had one hand in her coat pocket, but the one that was hanging onto her pocketbook was red from the cold.

"Where's yours?" she said, "You should be wearing gloves, and where's your scarf? I'll give you mine." She reached her hand up to untie her scarf.

"No! Now, Mother, don't do that! I won't put it on. I never wear scarves and the only time I wear gloves is if we go sliding, or I'm going to be out a long time. Now, don't give me your scarf. The bus will be here in a few minutes."

"You never listen," she said, but she said it softly, not mad the way she used to sound when I wouldn't listen to her. She didn't seem to get mad at anything anymore. She never said anything to Dad when he was drunk. Most of the time she stayed in bed when he came bumping in at one o'clock in the morning calling us to get up and "talk to the old man." I couldn't remember when the last time was when I heard her beg to stay home a little longer at the end of her visit. I didn't understand why she acted different, but I believed she still cared because sometimes I could hear her downstairs crying all by herself early in the morning on the day she was supposed to go back. I never went to her when she was crying because I didn't know what to say. I felt like that most of the time with her. Neither one of us talked for the rest of the trip home. It was just a few days until Christmas and the baby was already almost three weeks old.

Sometimes the holidays were hard to get through in our house. Dad would usually get us a Christmas tree, but he wouldn't get it until Christmas Eve because he always got a bonus check from the plating factory where he worked. Elsmarie and I learned that the best chance of having any money for the holidays was to show up at the shop Christmas party late in the afternoon.

There would be a long table covered with a white cloth and it would be full of all different kinds of food. Dad would be there with all of the people he worked with. The difference between him and everyone else is that they would look normal and be talking in normal voices and Dad would be talking too loud and trying to tell corny jokes. He'd make a big deal out of us coming and sometimes he'd make a remark about his kids being able to smell a little extra money, but he would give us each some. Usually, we could count on each of us getting a twenty-dollar-bill. He probably got a couple of hundred dollars for his bonus, plus his paycheck. He would have gone out at lunch and had a couple of drinks cashing his paycheck, but he had to go back to work for the party because that's when the bonuses were handed out.

The routine was that he'd give us money from his paycheck so we could do some shopping and get whatever we needed for our little celebration before the stores closed at five o'clock. It was during those few hours of having a little money to buy presents for Mother, Dad and each other that my sister and I could experience some Christmas joy. For me, I would get caught up in the pleasure and excitement that I would see on the faces of the other last-minute shoppers. Walking through the snow from store to store downtown on Main Street in Jamestown, knowing that I was going to buy something and take it home to wrap up for someone in my family, was fun. I loved the sound of the bells when I opened the doors to enter a store and the sounds of the Christmas carols coming over the loudspeakers as I looked over the tables and racks of possible gifts. A shirt for Dad and maybe a nightgown for Mother; Elsmarie was always the hardest person to buy for because I always wanted to get her something special.

Having Mother home at Christmas meant that she would go shopping, too. In a way, I was glad to have her, especially now that Elsmarie was married. My sister didn't have to do all of her shopping on Christmas Eve anymore, and besides, she had Peggy to take care of. Mother and I took the bus to Jamestown and got our money from Dad. He said he couldn't leave his party yet, but that he would meet us back home after he had done his shopping for us. I knew that we would be lucky if we saw him before eleven o'clock and that he would be too drunk to hold up his own head.

Mom and I went to town together and split up so she cold buy a present for me and I could buy hers. We agreed to meet at Murphy's Five and Dime in an hour. She said she wished we could go to the Catholic Church for Midnight Mass, but she knew we couldn't because we wouldn't have been able to get a bus home at that hour. She wanted to go to Fulton's Fish Market before we went home so she could buy salted fish to make Lute Fisk because it was one of Dad's favorite Christmas dishes. She had enough money to buy some Swedish Korv and a jar of Sill (pickled fish) and, for a while, she seemed to be excited like she used be. She wanted to go home right away after we finished getting everything. "We need to get home so I can cook supper before your father gets home."

We got on the bus at Third Street, carrying all of our packages. "Don't look in that one," she said pointing to one of the bags she set down at her feet. "I hope you like what I got for you," she smiled and put the tip of her tongue in that space where the teeth were missing. "And I hope I get supper cooked before you father gets home."

I wanted to believe that Dad would be home like he said he would. But I knew better. Why didn't Mother know better? How could she keep believing in him after all he'd put her through? I didn't say anything to her. On the ride home I thought about some of those long ago Christmases. I remembered chubby little blond boys with crew cuts dressed in velvet suits, toddling around Aunt Anna's big house on Christmas Eve. The bed in her spare room would be piled high with coats, and adults all dressed up would be sitting around all through the house talking softly and then laughing out loud as they held plates on their laps. The way the house smelled made you hungry and all you had to do was go in the kitchen and look anywhere to find trays of cookies, breads, meats and salads of every kind. Farmor would be sitting in the kitchen smiling, ready to help you put food on your plate. After everyone had eaten, we would all go into the big living room where the Christmas tree was and someone would start handing out presents, and everyone would get one.

Christmas Day was when we went to Aunt Jan's house. Grandma and Grandpa Stewart would be there and Mother's two brothers, Raymond and Dick, and their wives would be there. Uncle Ray had two girls almost the same age as Elsmarie and me, and Aunt Jan's mean boys would be there, too, but they had to be good because their father was home. Mother didn't have as many people on her side as there were on Daddy's side of the family, and there weren't as many different kinds of food to choose from, but it was nice to be with family and everyone seemed to have a good time. Daddy wouldn't drink when we were at Aunt Anna's house, but Grandpa Stewart, Daddy and my uncles drank on Christmas day at Aunt Jan's house. I wondered what happened to those days, and if Mother ever thought about them.

It was dark when we got back home to the little house in Celoron. We didn't have any time to waste because Elsmarie and Rodney were bringing the baby down at seven o'clock. They had gotten us a Christmas tree earlier in the week and we had already decorated it. All we had to do was wrap our presents and Mother was going to cook our supper. She took her gifts upstairs and wrapped them in her bedroom while I wrapped mine downstairs. It didn't take long and our little tree had gifts underneath and was looking good. We had also bought some silver icicles and I put them on the tree while Mother went in the kitchen to start the meal.

Before long, Mother had the potatoes peeled and cooking on the stove, and the water was boiling for the Korv. She took out another cooking pot and started to make her white sauce for the Lute Fisk and then Elsmarie and Rodney arrived with little Peggy. "Something smells good, Mother. What's cooking?" Elsmarie sounded happy and I was glad to hear her say nice things to Mother.

"Your father will be home soon," Mother said as she pulled dishes out of the cupboard. "And then we'll eat."

"Yeah, well, we're not waiting for him, Mother." Elsmarie helped with the table while I unwrapped little Peggy from her blankets and bunting. Rodney didn't say anything. Most of the time he didn't talk around us.

"We can wait a little, can't we?" Mother looked nervous.

"We can wait until the food is cooked, but we're not waiting any longer than that." Elsmarie was frustrated and determined. "Ma, you know how he is. He won't be home tonight until all the bars close up. I'm not waiting around for him to come home and spoil another

Christmas. And I'm not having Peggy listen to his drunken excuses for why he didn't make it."

"Okay," Mother said, "You've got to get the baby home. You eat and I'll wait for your father."

"Look, Mother, we came down to eat with you and Eileen. Rodney's mother has all kinds of food up at their house, but I wanted to eat with you. Now, come on! If you don't sit down and eat with us, then we might as well go now."

"I'll sit down with you, but I'm going to wait and eat with your father." Mother wasn't going to budge and neither was Elsmarie.

"Well, have a Merry Christmas, then! We're might as well go now." Elsmarie was sitting next to the baby sleeping on the couch and was stuffing her little arms back into the little pink quilted bunting jacket. "I can't take this anymore, Mother. It's been going on for as long as I can remember, but I'm going to enjoy Christmas this year!" Having finished bundling the baby, she grabbed her own coat and got into it. Rodney stood up and picked up his jacket, still not saying a word. "There's presents for all of you in the bag over by the tree," she said, and the little family disappeared out the door.

Mother sat silently at the kitchen table. She wasn't crying and she didn't look mad. She just sat there. I had seen her look that way many times over the years. Something bad would happen and she would just sit quietly. I wondered what she was thinking about, but I didn't ask.

I sat down at the table, too. "They didn't take their presents," I said. After what seemed like a long silence, I said, "I'll turn on the television. Maybe there's a Christmas program on for us to watch."

"I hope they have Midnight Mass on the television tonight." she said. "It's so pretty. "A Christmas Carol" was on T.V. and we watched some of that together. When it got to be about nine o'clock, I went out to the kitchen because I was hungry. "Wait a minute," she said when I first started to take some food. "I'll heat that up for you. It won't take long."

Before long, the potatoes, Korv and Lute Fisk were hot again and she fixed herself a plate, too. We ate in front of the television so we could finish watching the movie. I was glad she was home. We watched until Dad came in. He was so blasted that he couldn't make it all the way across the room to the couch and he had to flop down in the chair by the door. He managed to mumble a few things that no one could understand anyway before his head fell back, his chin fell down and he was out for the night. I helped Mother clear away the dishes and put the leftover food away and we decided to wait until morning for presents.

"Maybe we can walk up to Elsmarie's tomorrow morning and bring their presents up to them," Mother said as we were cleaning up.

"Okay." I said. Tomorrow was going to be a better day.

XI

Teenagers are self-centered by design and I was no exception. It was a time for me when worries about the size of my chest occupied most of my thoughts; that and growing a backside big enough to fill out a straight skirt and then finding a boyfriend were more important than anything. Dad could have drunk the Imperial Hotel dry for all I cared during those early teenage years and Mom became more important again as figment of my imagination, than she was as a real person. I can't imagine how difficult those years must have been for her to have her youngest child, and the only child left in the home, regarding her with so little interest that I can't remember answering her letters during that time. It must have been then that she stopped trying to contact me. It was 1958 and I was fourteen years old.

Things started looking up when I was fourteen. I finally had a reason to be wearing my size 32A bra and I had managed to buy enough clothes so I could wear something clean every day of the week and do laundry only on Saturdays. I had more offers for babysitting jobs than I could handle on the weekends, so I was able to tell Mr. and Mrs. Jimmy Drake that I couldn't babysit for their six kids anymore. That left my school nights free to get to bed at a decent hour and pretty much make it to school every day. Probably the best thing of all was that I had a very best friend.

Diane and I were both misfits for very different reasons. I could not blend into my class at Southwestern Central because I was certainly the skinniest and probably the poorest girl in the entire class; I thought there was one skinnier than me when I was in sixth grade for a while, but she moved away. It also didn't help my popularity to be the kid that lived in that awful house down on that section of the Boulevard where no one went unless they had business there. Good people didn't have business at Nelson's Cafe, the liquor store, Howard's Second Hand Store or Glamor Manor.

Diane was a misfit because she was, without question, the prettiest girl in our eighth grade class. She never went through an awkward stage. She never had a pimple on her face and her complexion was so pretty that some of the girls thought she wore makeup before anyone else and the truth was that her parents wouldn't let her and she didn't need it. She had honey-colored hair and big green eyes with long dark lashes and she had a good figure. She needed a regular bra when the rest of us were just daydreaming about training bras.

Most of the junior high girls avoided Diane. After all, if you can't get boys from your own class who have pimples all over their faces and are shorter than you to show any interest, then it doesn't help to see someone your age turning down sophomore and junior football players. Maybe she was just tired of being lonely, too, or maybe she really saw something in me worth liking, but, for whatever reason, she wanted to be my friend. I never thought that it was because she felt sorry for me; if she did she covered it up really well. We first met outside of school one afternoon when she and her younger brother, Denny, and some of his friends were across the street at the picnic grove playing baseball. She called me over and said, "How about if you and I play baseball against my brother and his creepy little friends? If I don't play with him he'll go home crying to my mother that I wouldn't play with him."

Saying yes to that offer was one of the best decisions I ever made. It was hard for me to believe that I could be a best friend for someone as nice as Diane, but it certainly seemed that we were good for each other. We started spending as much time together as her mother would allow. She lived three blocks away from me upstairs of a two-family house that her parents owned. Many of the houses on Conewango Street had three floors and that was the way Diane's was. They had a big living room and kitchen and bath on the second floor and three bedrooms separated by a short hall on the third floor. Diane's room was small, but really pretty, with matching curtains and bedspread. She had a stack of dolls and stuffed animals from her childhood stashed in one corner and had decorated her walls with Ricky Nelson and Elvis Presley posters. She had her own little record player in her room that played forty-five speed records and we spent hours in there with her door closed, listening to music and talking endlessly about boys.

I never heard Diane say anything bad about anyone except maybe how mean some boys were and how stupid some of them acted. I knew that some of the other girls in school talked about her, and one time Barbara said to me, "I wouldn't hang around with Diane if I were you. You're going to get a bad reputation because you ought to know why so many boys hang around her all the time."

"You're wrong," I said, "she's not like that; and the reason the boys hang around her is because she's pretty and you shouldn't talk about people when you don't know them." It felt good to stick up for my friend, especially when everything I said was true. I thought I might tell Diane what Barbara said, but I didn't. Why take a chance on hurting her feelings when she was so nice about everyone else.

Diane never asked why I didn't invite her to my house, and she never asked about my family. I never offered to tell her anything about any of that because I guess it felt better to have a place to get away from it. When I was with Diane, I didn't feel like I was the daughter of the drunk and the woman in the nuthouse. I was just a teenager, like everyone else. To make things even better, Elsmarie and Rodney had moved out of his parents' apartment to a little house just two doors down from Diane. They had fixed it up really cute and when I was babysitting little Peggy, I could actually invite Diane into that little house and feel proud. Proud of the way the house looked and that I had a beautiful little niece as well. I felt like I had something to contribute to our friendship.

Diane teased her little brother, but really only in self-defense because he was a little brat. She was really good with little kids. She took care of her Aunt Janet and Uncle Joe's kids, Eddie and Nadine, lots of times and she was better with Peggy than I was. Sometimes when I was babysitting for my sister, I couldn't get Peggy to stop crying and Diane could pick her up and she'd calm right down. She just had a way about her.

At first when I started spending so much time at Diane's, I felt like her mother didn't really like me. One time when she came home from work and saw me there, she said, "Don't you ever have to go home?"

I started to leave right away and Diane said, "Don't worry about what she said. She's in a bad mood today. She's probably got her period or something." Her mother never said anything like that again to me so maybe Diane was right about her being in a bad mood.

Diane wasn't allowed to go on dates until she was sixteen, even though she had plenty of offers. I didn't go out on dates either, but that was because I didn't have any offers. But there was a boy who lived in one of the apartments at Rodney's parents' house that summer that I was fourteen who was interested in me. David was fourteen, too, and while I would have preferred the attentions of an older boy, someone at least fifteen, it was very nice to have a boyfriend. He might have been an inch or two taller than me and he was skinny, too, but he wasn't bad looking and he wore nice clothes and kept his hair like the other boys; a crew-cut top, but long on the sides, slicked back to a duck tail. He was kind of shy as far as talking, but liked to hold hands and even experiment with kissing. Diane had a little experience at kissing thanks to a sophomore boy who lived in Celoron and showed up everywhere that she was for a long time. Anyway, when I told her about kissing David, she was able to offer some expert advice. "How was it?" she asked.

"Well, it really didn't do much for me," I said. "He just kind of pressed his lips against mine and wanted to just keep doing that and, after a while, it just felt boring and stupid. I hope that's not all there is to it."

Diane looked puzzled and thoughtful and then she said, "Next time, open your mouth a little and try to get him to do the same thing."

"Is that what we're supposed to do?"

"No wonder it was boring." Diane gave me an ah-hah look. "I don't know if you're supposed to or not, but I found out it makes kissing a whole lot better!"

David was living with his aunt and uncle who were very strict with him, but they adored my sister and thought she could do no wrong, so when David wanted to babysit with me at Elsmarie's house, they agreed. They probably thought we were both so nice and innocent that we would spend the evening playing Dominoes. Well, that's kind of what we told them we were going to do. If they had known that we were going to spend the evening practicing our kissing and studying the anatomy section of Elsmarie's *Family Medical Guide*, David would not have been allowed out.

Diane was right. Kissing with our mouths open a little did make all the difference in the world. David and I kissed until we were both dizzy that next Saturday night. David's hands started roaming around and I stopped him. Part of the reason I didn't let him go on was because I was going to prove my Dad was wrong when he'd come home drunk and say, "It won't be long and you'll do the same as your sister, and you'll get pregnant by some boy." He would always ask me the same thing, "Tell me something, are you still a virgin?" I got so I hated the question. The other reason I wouldn't let David go any farther was because I wasn't ready for anything more.

I knew what I was doing, even though Dad made me feel dirty when he was drunk and asked me all those questions about sex and practically accused me of doing things I hadn't even thought of before. He never took those things back when he was sober, so I guess that's what he really thought about me. He acted like sex was all that girls were good for and that's all they wanted to do was make out with a boy. Sure, Diane and I talked about boys and sex a lot and I suppose we were curious. But we thought about lots of other things, too. We would get up a bunch of kids and play softball at the picnic grove sometimes in the afternoons after school and we played Kick the Can at night. We rode our bikes up to Lakewood Beach in the summer so we could go swimming and sat for hours at Diane's house playing cards or chess.

In the winter months, we went sliding down Miller's hill. The Millers were a nice older couple who had a great hill at the side of their house and they let all the kids in the neighborhood come and slide whenever they wanted to. It didn't matter if you didn't have a sled because a piece of cardboard worked great, and what was better was a round metal tray. We used to go to the back doors of the beer joints and beg them for their old beer trays because they worked great for sliding. Sometimes, Nancy and Janice would go with Diane and me and we would just walk around for hours in the winter talking; the air was so cold at times that the insides of our nostrils felt icy and our fingers and toes would get numb, but we just hated to give it up and go in.

Eventually, I would have to go home. Usually I would go home at suppertime just like everyone else. As soon as someone said, "Man, I better get home for supper, or my mother will kill me," I would say, "Oh, me too. I don't want to get in trouble either, so I'll see you later." Whatever the other kids had to do, I said I had to do the same. No one questioned me about it.

If it was a Sunday evening, or one of Dad's other sober evenings, he would look away from the television and at me long enough to ask, "Where have you been all day? I cooked supper."

"I know, Dad, that's why I came home. I've just been out sliding with my friends, that's all. I'll set the table." As long as I followed the schedules that Diane and the other kids had to keep, he couldn't really say much because I was home for supper and in at a decent hour if I went anywhere in the evenings. I was not ashamed of anything I was doing when I was out, and if he wanted to check up on me, he could anytime. As we got older, we started asking for permission to go to the skating rink in the evenings.

Diane's parents wouldn't allow her to go skating in the evenings. They wouldn't let her go much of anywhere after supper. Sometimes, on Thursday nights when I knew that Dad wouldn't be home anyway, I started going skating. I wasn't very good at it and it kind of scared me to be out on that skating floor, I was afraid that I would fall down and everyone would look at me. It seemed like the girls who were there spent most of their time in the girls' bathroom, smoking, fixing their make up and hair and talking about boys. I felt pretty left out of things. There weren't as many Celoron kids as I thought would be at the rink, so I really didn't have a friend to hang around with; most of the kids came up from Jamestown on the bus. I wanted to learn how to skate and it was extra hard to do if you had to keep renting your skates because you usually ended up with a different pair every time you went. After I'd been going a couple of weeks, Mr. Zimmer, the owner, offered to sell me a pair of used skates. He said I could pay a little each week if I needed to until they were paid up. I took him up on it and it got a little easier, but even though I went a lot, I never really had a good time and I never felt like I belonged.

During the summer between eighth and ninth grade, all any of us could talk about was whether or not we would be tapped by a sorority. There were three sororities at Southwestern Central School. None of us in Celoron thought we would be invited to join Phi Delta Tau because the girls in that one were all the rich kids from Lakewood whose fathers were doctors, lawyers, or dentists. Those girls had enough money so that even if they weren't cute, they made up for it with great clothes, an expensive haircut and a confident attitude. Rho Delta Phi was the in-between group for the middle-class kids who were cute and popular even if they weren't rich. The third one was Kappa Zeta Chi and it was considered kind of low-class by the kids in the other two sororities. You had to practically be a zombie not to get invited into that one, but the girls were all pretty nice, it wasn't like they were just a bunch of rough girls like some of the ones that came from Jamestown to the skating rink.

"I'll bet we both get a bid to join Kappa Zeta Chi," Diane said. "I'll join if they ask me, I like the kids in that sorority best. They don't act like they think they're better than everyone else."

"I probably won't get asked by anyone, but you'll get a bid from Rho Delta Phi, " I said.

"Well, if they don't ask you, then I'm not joining," she said.

"Don't be dumb, you should be in Rho Del. If they don't give you a bid, then there's something wrong with them." Diane tried out for Junior varsity cheerleading and she made it without any trouble. She wanted me to try out, but I didn't because even though I had filled out some, I was still skinny and not very athletic. Just thinking about trying out made my heart pound and my mouth get dry.

That fall after school started, we learned that I was right in my prediction that Rho Delta Phi would give a bid to Diane, and to my surprise, Kappa Zeta Chi gave me a bid. We each joined the sorority that tapped us. We were both a little sad that we couldn't be together, but as our friendship went on, it just became stronger and we found that we were still best friends even when we were going in different directions. Diane was busy lots of the times with cheerleading practice and games and that gave me more time to babysit for my little niece and for the other families that used me when my sister didn't need me. I was able to earn money for more clothes, shoes and other things I needed.

Things at home didn't get any better, but it didn't matter as much anymore. I didn't have to sit staring out the window at the street below, praying that I'd see my father staggering up the street towards home, or that the next car would stop down in front of the house and let him out. I went to bed when I was tired whether he was home or not. I'd still have to get up and listen to his drunk stories, sometimes, but if it wasn't so late that the television had signed off, I'd turn it on and have the late show on while he rambled on about the same things over and over. One Friday night, he didn't come home at all and I didn't even know it until Elsmarie woke me up the next morning.

"Eileen, come down here. I'm so sorry you've been here by yourself all night!" She was standing at the bottom of the stairs and she was calling up to me because I was still in bed. She was really mad. "Dad called me from Oil City, Pennsylvania. Somehow he ended up down there, drunk and he said whoever he was with rolled him and he's stranded. I've got to go down to his job and see if they'll give me some money to send to him so he can get home."

I got up and went downstairs. "I'm sorry you have to go through all that to get him that money, but don't feel bad for me, I didn't even know that he didn't come home. I went to sleep early last night."

"Well, damn it!" He shouldn't be leaving my kid sister alone while he's off so blasted that he can't even get home. I'm so damn sick and tired of the way he acts! We ought to just leave him down there. Anyway, I wanted to be sure you're okay and let you know where he is." With that she stormed out of the house. It was a much bigger deal to her than it was to me. I went back to bed as soon as she pulled out of the driveway. It seemed especially peaceful knowing where Dad was and that he was safe, but having him somewhere else besides home.

I was never surprised about much of anything that Dad said or did. One Friday night, he surprised me by bursting in the house two hours earlier than the time he usually came in. "Do I have clean shirt in the closet?" he asked. His face was twisted into a sneer and he kind of weaved a little as he stood in the doorway so I knew he was pretty smashed.

116

"Yeah," I said, "I think there's one or two up there. Why?"

"Will you go get one for me? I'll show that son of a bitch that I have clean shirts!" he said, while holding onto the back of the chair.

I was glad to go up and get one; especially if that meant he was going back out. I was planning on watching the late show on television and I sure didn't want to listen to him. I could hear him mumbling to himself as I came back downstairs with a shirt on a hanger.

"I'll show that son of a bitch that he can't call me a bum!" He was really mad at someone who had apparently hurt his feelings. "I told him I could get a clean shirt anytime I wanted to." I looked at the shirt he was pulling off that he had worn to work that morning and he had spilled something all over the front. I suppose the other drunk was giving him a hard time about it so he was settling it. I wasn't all that worried about him, even though he was in bad shape because he wasn't driving and he didn't have far to walk to get back to the bar. I'd be able to watch the late show without being interrupted because as bad off as he was just then, I knew he'd pass out right after he got back home.

Mother was the one who still surprised me. When she was on a home visit, I worried sometimes if she would be too lonely left on her own so much, now that I had friends and something to do all the time, but she was just fine. Lots of times I'd come home after being at Diane's house, or with sorority sisters and she would be just getting home herself. It didn't matter what the weather was, she'd get dressed up as much as she could and go downtown. On Wednesdays, she'd go to the Salvation Army to the Ladies Aid meeting.

She'd say, "You should have seen how nice your Aunt Anna looked. They just got back from Florida, you know. She had on a navy blue coat and a matching hat... and the hat perfect for her face."

"Mother," I'd say. "How can you say such nice things about relatives who've never done anything nice for you?"

"Listen to the way you talk!" she'd say. "She's your father's sister!"

I didn't argue with her very much anymore because I didn't want to make her feel bad. I was better off not paying much attention to the things she said, but it turned out that Mother had places to go, too. If she didn't go to the Ladies Aid, she could visit her mother or her sister and sometimes she said she enjoyed just looking at all the things in the stores downtown. Usually she had enough money for the bus, but one day I got home and she wasn't there yet. I was getting worried because it was winter and it was getting dark and she wasn't usually gone that long. We had a phone then, but she didn't call and I was just about ready to get a hold of Elsmarie to let her know about Mom being so late, when she came in. The temperature had really dropped once the sun went down and it was quite cold outside. "Mother!" You're freezing! Where have you been?"

"I went to Ladies Aid." She stood in front of the gas space heater in the living room and held her hands over it to try to warm them. They were bright red from the cold and so was her face. It almost looked like there were ice crystals on her eyebrows. "I took the bus down," she said, "but I must have dropped some of my change somewhere, because after I walked back up to Third Street to get the bus home, I saw that I didn't have enough money, so I walked home."

"Why didn't you call Elsmarie, Mother? She would have gone down to get you." I wanted to cry and it made me mad.

"I didn't think it was going to turn so cold. It's not a bad walk in nice weather," she said, "I've done it before, and besides, I should have kept better track of my money."

It was almost five miles to Jamestown. I only went there when I had saved enough babysitting money so I could buy some clothes, or if Diane and I went to the movies, so I didn't know why Mother would go all that way just to have something to do on a freezing cold winter day, but in a way I did understand. Dad had his drinking, Elsmarie had Rodney and the baby, I had my friends and school, and Mother had to have something, too. I just hoped she wouldn't ever walk that far again in the cold. None of us knew it then, but within a few months, we would be leaving Celoron and moving back to Jamestown. It would be one of the hardest moves I ever had to make.

XII

Spring and summer went by quickly that year. For the most part I still didn't think about Mother or Dad. I had my friends and a life outside of our little house. I was able to escape to the world of the teenager where days were occupied with school gossip about who was going steady or had broken up, school sports and the endless passing of hastily written notes that were slipped under desks from one pair of hands to another while a teacher droned on in front of the classroom. Being accepted meant everything; it was more important than my family, my grades and my future. I would have given anything to be popular then. I would love to have walked down the hall with a tall, handsome boy's arm close around me and known just when to flip my hair back and say clever things. I felt like I was doing all right, though, I had a few good friends (mostly girls) and a couple of boys who liked me even though they were so unpopular I would have been embarrassed to be seen with them. I was in chorus and drama club and most of my classes were easy, except for algebra, which I didn't get at all. I certainly would not have been considered a popular girl, but people didn't turn away from me if I walked up to them and I don't think anyone made faces behind my back.

Diane started seeing one of the most popular football players on the varsity team. He had been trying to date her since she was in the eighth grade. Her parents didn't exactly let her start dating, but because she was a cheerleader and he was the star quarterback, they were bound to find time to be together. There was always a dance after the home games and by that summer he had been at Di's house enough so her parents felt comfortable enough to let her go out with him on his boat. Roger lived in Lakewood and was one of those beautiful tanned young men who always seemed to have a boat and was great at water skiing. Who could blame Diane for falling for a guy like that?

With David gone back to live in Falconer, we didn't see much of each other, so I dated Diane's cousin for a while. He was a couple of years older and it was harder to keep him from getting carried away. He was very good at kissing, but the more we kissed, the more he begged me to let him do it. I wasn't ready. I met a boy at the skating rink named Gary. He had red hair and really broad shoulders and he always smelled great. I thought he was very good looking. One night he asked me to skate with him and then he invited me to go on a date with him sometime. I thought it was too good to be true that he could really like me. As it turned out, it was too good to be true because the date turned out to be a drive-in movie and nothing more than a wrestling match. He finally got so mad at me because I wouldn't let him make out with me that he took me home and after I got out of the car he drove off spinning his tires. So much for him. There were a couple of other boys in Celoron who were very friendly to me and I felt good about their friendship.

Usually, I was prepared for anything Dad did; he rarely surprised me anymore. I knew not to pay attention to his remorseful promises on Sunday mornings that he was never going to drink again. He would drink again, as soon as Thursday and his paycheck arrived. I learned to expect the worst at Christmas and the week of the Fourth of July when his shop bonuses came in. But I was not prepared for his announcement that Saturday morning in late October. For one thing it was strange that he was home; usually he worked on Saturday mornings and then he'd finish off the day drinking. Not only was he home, but he was sober and he was in the kitchen wrapping our dishes in newspaper and packing them in a box that was open front of him.

"What are you doing?" I asked, wondering if he was planning on leaving me because he hadn't said a word to me about planning to pack.

"We're moving," he said. I couldn't see the expression on his face in the dim kitchen. Even on the sunniest days, we had to burn the kitchen light because the only window was in the top half of the side door and it didn't let in any light at all. He didn't look up.

"When?" I asked, wondering if he was drunk this early in the day.

My throat was getting tight and my stomach felt funny.

"Now," he answered without looking at me. "We're moving over the weekend." Even though I couldn't see his face, I knew he was sober because his words were clear and even.

I couldn't believe what I was hearing, "Where are we going?"

"We're moving to Jamestown," he said, still without looking at me.

"I can't leave Celoron now!" I had to sit down. I suddenly felt weak. "I've made a life here, Dad. Don't make me move now! Please, don't do this!"

"It's already done. I've got a place for us down on Eighth Street. It's nicer than anything we've had in a long time. We can't stay here anymore."

"What about school?" I was yelling now, "What about the friends I've made? So you didn't pay the rent, right?"

"They have schools in Jamestown. And you can visit your friends, you know..." He sounded frustrated, and maybe even sorry. "Anyway, I can't do anything about it now and I don't want to hear any more about it! Now, you're going to have to help with the packing. I can't do it all alone."

I usually never cried anymore, but I cried all that day as I packed up our belongings. It didn't take long because we didn't have that much. The only glassware we had, other than the dishes, were the ashtrays on the coffee table in the living room. We had a few lamps and some pictures on the walls that Mother had picked up at the second-hand store. There was a little artificial flower arrangement, our photo albums and our clothes. We had just a few towels and the sheets we had on our beds, so the "linens" didn't take up much room. When we moved to this house on the Boulevard, six years earlier, Dad had been forced to buy beds for Elsmarie and me; all of the rest of the furniture belonged to the landlady. I wondered how the beds were going to be moved; they weren't going to fit in the backseat of the car he had bought a few weeks earlier.

By early evening, everything was packed and we waited until one of Dad's drinking buddies showed up with a small truck. We moved away from Celoron the same way we moved in six years ago; in the night. I didn't try to see Diane before we left because I knew that if

I tried to say goodbye to her I would cry. As close as we had become, we still didn't cry in front of each other. It would be easier on both of us to call her from Jamestown.

I saw where we were to live in Jamestown for the first time as I carried my small box of personal things in. He was right about one thing: It was nicest place I'd ever lived. We had one whole side of a duplex. We had a living room, dining room and kitchen downstairs with a stairway off the dining room. The bathroom was at the top of the stairs and there were three bedrooms that opened up from a long hall. I couldn't believe there was actually a hall separating the bedrooms. I couldn't help but like the place after all the dumps we'd lived in all my life. It was actually pleasant with high ceilings and tall windows and decent woodwork around the doors and windows. The rooms had clean-looking wallpaper with flowers like Aunt Mildred's house and the downstairs was furnished okay. The buffet in the dining room looked like it matched the table and the couch and chair in the living room were also a matched set and you might not feel like you should throw an old sheet or something on the furniture before you could sit down. There was a front porch and a little back entrance way that led to a small yard. The only rooms that weren't furnished were the two smaller bedrooms, which worked out fine because we had Elsmarie's and my twin beds to go in those rooms.

It was such an improvement over the other places that I would have been happy instead of sad over the loss of my life in Celoron. Maybe what Dad and Elsmarie said was true and I was "just selfish to not be happy that we could all live in a better place!" Elsmarie was back, with Peggy, to live with us. She and Rodney had been having serious problems for some time.

In the six years that I attended Southwestern Central School System I never heard a student talk back to a teacher, and I never saw a fight. On my first day as a student at the Jamestown Public School System I saw a fight involving several girls who scratched one another's faces, and pulled each other's hair as they shouted words that I had only heard my father use just before he passed out drunk. The next day I saw two students throw a book at the librarian from the hall. My first instincts that the girls from Jamestown who came to Celoron to skate were not people I wanted as friends were correct. Now, they were my classmates.

Elsmarie had met someone who promised to love and protect her forever and she spent all of her time with her new boyfriend. Dad had the convenience of two beer joints within a short walking distance from the new place, and aside from phone calls to Diane, I was left alone to try to figure out what to do next. Nothing seemed to be working out very well for me. I had gotten into the habit of getting up to hear Dad's reasons for getting drunk again which probably made him feel better, but wasn't doing anything for me. For the first time in a long time, I was beginning to really miss Ma.

The weather began to turn cold as winter set in and Mother finally got to come home to see the new place. She said it was nice and she was glad to be closer to her mother's apartment and to the Salvation Army so she could attend services. We were also close enough to walk to a large Catholic Church and she said she would be going to Midnight Mass on Christmas Eve. Mother didn't talk very much anymore about anything. She'd mention who she saw at Ladies Aid, or if she went to town and saw anyone we might know she would mention them, sometimes describing their outfits if she thought they looked particularly nice. When it was time for her to go back, she had to take herself back on the Greyhound Bus because something had happened to Dad's car. No one thought it was particularly strange that a mental patient was capable of getting herself back to the hospital. Usually, I wouldn't have thought it strange, either, but this time was different.

Dad couldn't get himself home from Fish's Cafe just two blocks up the road on his own on payday without help. I just couldn't figure out how it could be okay for Dad, who was supposed to be the responsible one, to have to take a taxi for a two-block ride because he was too drunk to walk and still be considered the one who was sane. I decided that I was going to Helmuth and talk to Mother's doctor to find out why she was still being kept there. I wanted to know what was wrong with her, and just when the doctor thought she might be well enough to come home. It was time someone in the family got some answers. I had tried talking to Dad one night after he came home. I waited up until the taxi pulled up in front of the house after his favorite bar had closed. It took several minutes for him to actually get into the house. First he had to maneuver the curb and then stagger up the porch steps. It would be another wait while he fumbled for his key and managed to aim straight enough to get in the lock. Eventually, he would burst in the door and bob and weave his way over to the dining room table where he would flop down with a thud.

"Where've you been, Dad?" I asked, even though I already knew. Dad was predictable.

"I went up to Fish's to see a man about a horse," he said, and laughed, it was one of his own favorite one-liners.

"Why can't Ma come home for good?" I asked. "What does she do that makes everyone believe she's crazy?"

Dad had been talking with his eyes mostly closed and his head propped up on his elbow.

"I guess you think it's been easy taking care of you girls with my wife in the nuthouse." Every time his head would start to fall over, he'd wake up just in time before it went straight down to the table and jerk himself up straight.

"Dad," I said, "just what is wrong with Mother? I mean, no one ever says anything about what her problem is. Do you know?"

He peered at me through his half-shut eyes. "Well, you know how she is!" he said, "You heard the way she used to scream at me and throw things at me. She's crazy!"

"Yes, but Dad, you just said it yourself. She used to do those things, but I haven't heard her do that in years." I was starting to yell. "So what's supposed to be wrong, now?"

"Well, they haven't let her out, have they? That ought to be your answer. If she wasn't nuts, then they'd let her out." He took a long drink from the can of beer he brought out of his coat pocket and set it down on the table. "I've got to lie down." He shoved his chair back, almost toppling it, staggered over to the couch and collapsed on it.

I called the hospital and made arrangements to see Mother's doctor. I wasn't asked about my age and I didn't volunteer, which probably explained the surprised expression on the faces of the office staff when I arrived promptly for my appointment. "Should we wait for someone else?" The middle-aged secretary looked beyond me towards the elevator, "Is someone parking the car, perhaps?" She looked back at me with raised eyebrows, but still smiling quite pleasantly.

I always had the idea that the doctors at the institution where Mom was kept were totally in charge of all of the care provided. "We'll have to ask the doctor," was always the answer given by nurses, or other staff working there no matter what the question was about a patient; usually, the question was about permission for a home visit, "If you'd care to hold, we'll check with her doctor," would come the crisp reply on the other end of the phone.

The voice would be back in no time at all, "The doctor said that will be fine. When will you be picking her up so we can notify them downstairs?"

I was always very impressed by the fact that the doctor always seemed to be available to make decisions about Mom whenever we called. How could anyone question such efficiency and dedication as shown by the doctors at Helmuth? And now, here I was about to see one of those psychiatric giants face to face. Suddenly, I felt small and vulnerable and too young to be here, but it was too late for those thoughts now.

"No," I said, "I made the appointment." Again, I wished I wasn't so skinny and I wondered if I should have worn a dress, or a skirt instead of slacks and a sweater. I had a pleated skirt that made me look fatter.

"Well then, come this way," she said, still smiling, and took me through a short hall where there were several doors with gold name plates, and stopped at one. "He's right in here and he's expecting you." She tapped lightly on the door and then opened it.

A man, who looked much younger than my father, sat behind the biggest desk I had ever seen. "Hello. Hello," he said, and then he stood up and gestured towards a chair. "Sit. Sit." He was smiling broadly. He wore a tweed suit and green tie with a sweater underneath the coat. He had a mustache and a beard that covered only his chin, making his face look long and pointed. His name plate was on the corner of the desk and I tried to sound out the long name that was on it. I decided I would have to refer to him as Dr. G. "Why are you here? Why are you here?" he asked.

I wondered at first why he repeated everything he said, but I soon learned that he was trying to be clear to me. There was a definite language barrier between us.

"My mother has been here since I was four years old," I said, "and I would like to know what's wrong with her and how long she will have to stay here."

He opened the folder in front of him and referred to it. "Ah," he said, "she was very ill when she came in. We gave her many shock treatments." He looked back at me and smiled again.

"Does she still have them?" I asked, almost afraid of his answer.

He looked again at the folder. "No, not in many years." He smiled. I had to listen very closely to understand him because his accent was so thick. It was probably German, or Austrian. I couldn't tell. It could have been Polish or Hungarian.

"Then why is she still here?" I repeated my question. "Do you know the lady I'm talking about?" I asked as he studied the folder again.

He shrugged his shoulders and gestured. "I have many patients," he said. "I can't know them all."

"How long have you been her doctor?" I asked carefully, pronouncing each word so he would understand my question.

He shrugged his shoulders and gestured, "I don't know the answer to your questions. I have been in this Country not even a year. Maybe she'll be well next year, huh? I must go now." And he stood up and gestured towards the door to let me know our meeting was over.

I got up and started for the door, then remembered about taking Mother with me that day, so I turned and said, "I would like to take my mother back with me for a visit."

"Yes. You make the arrangements with the secretary at the desk. That's fine. That's fine." He gave a little bow and kept smiling.

At the desk I asked the secretary, "Did the doctor just call you on the phone, or something?"

She was working on something at the typewriter, but looked up at me with a puzzled expression, "No. Was he supposed to tell me something?"

"Well, it's just that I asked him if I could take my mother home with me for a visit," I answered, wondering if she would call him.

"Oh, sure. That'll be fine," she said. "Did you want her for one week, or two?" She jotted something down on her desk calendar and smiled at me.

"Let's say two. I guess." I felt totally confused and more than a little foolish. So that was how the big decisions were made about Mom's home visits; the secretary decided. I wondered what she did while I was on hold all those times; maybe filed her nails, or went for a coffee. Maybe she couldn't ask the doctor because she couldn't understand him any better than I could.

"Fine! I'll put her down for two weeks," she said brightly. And then, "I'll call downstairs and tell them to let your mother know."

On the bus ride home, I said, "I saw your doctor, Mom."

"Did you? Which one did you see? I've had so many I wouldn't know one from the other anymore."

"Mom..." I was choosing my words carefully, because I thought that, surely, she'd clear up my confusion. "Do you have more than one doctor at a time? Like maybe one that you talk to; you know about how you're doing and when you might go home?"

"No," she said, "I don't have anyone who talks to me like that, Oh, once in a while, I'll talk to one of the nurses about going home. Why?"

"Well, Mom, I don't understand why you have to stay there." I could feel myself getting upset and mad, but I didn't know who to be mad at.

"I can't go home till someone signs me out. It's the law," she said. "When someone signs you in, then someone has to sign you out. The man who runs the laundry has been there twenty years, or more and he can't get out either. Imagine it," she said, "he's in charge of the whole laundry, but he can't leave the hospital grounds."

"So Dad could sign you out if he wanted to." I was getting a headache just thinking about it.

"I don't know anymore if he could. And I don't know if I could take it anymore," she said and tears started forming in her eyes. "Let's talk about something else."

I didn't understand it, and I didn't think I ever would. I couldn't

127

think about this family anymore. I needed to think about getting out. Someday I would meet a wonderful man who would ask me to marry him and he would never drink or cause any problems. We would have children and our family would be very happy. All I had to do was hang on a little while longer and my life would start to get better.

When I visited Diane, I learned that she and Roger were going steady and that they were in love. They were also going farther and farther with making out. She was scared but happy, and she felt like it wouldn't be long before they would go all the way. I wasn't jealous in the way that I didn't want her to be in love, because she deserved someone special like Roger and I was happy for her. I just wondered when it would be my turn. I was tired of being lonely.

With Diane in Celoron and wrapped up with Roger, I started spending time with one of the girls in Jamestown. Jackie was short and cute with a pixie look to her. She was also tougher than anyone I had ever met. She was always chewing gum, which she cracked all the time. I had seen her at school, but I didn't think she ever noticed me. She usually had a boy with her and she was always laughing and talking in a loud voice. The boys seemed to love her. We started skipping school together. In fact, that's how we met; skipping school and showing up at the drugstore when we were supposed to be in school. I was buying a pack of cigarettes.

"Hey," she said, coming from the aisle behind me, "Don't we go to the same school?" and then she burst out laughing, which she did no matter who she was with.

I had never been much for giggling, or bursting out laughing a lot, but I often wished I could be more outgoing. "I guess you wouldn't believe that I had to get up out of a sick-bed to come and buy medicine, would you?" I said with a smile, knowing we had just discovered each other skipping school.

"Sure I would, because I'm doing the same thing." She faked a coughing fit which ended up in another burst of laughter. We ended up going to her house, which, by the way, looked dirtier than any of the places I'd ever lived in. If you could look past the dusty, cluttered tables in the living room, you could see that they had some really nice furniture and a thick shag rug on the floor that was mostly covered with dirty socks and stacks of old newspapers and magazines. The kitchen was worse, with dirty dishes in the sink, on the sink drainboard, and all over the table, as well. There were cereal bowls with soured milk in the bottoms and plates that looked like they had old spaghetti stuck to them. The whole place smelled like soured milk and spoiled food. I almost didn't want to sit down. "Don't mind the mess," she said cheerfully. "My old lady has to work two jobs to keep my old man in booze, so nothing much gets done around here. Oh, I'm supposed to clean up, but I can't do that when I'm in school all day, can I?" She burst out with that laugh of hers again and told me to come in her bedroom and check out her collection of Elvis records.

I had never heard anyone speak so openly the way she did about her dad's drinking and I'd never heard a girl swear so much. I wondered if I would dare to tell her about my dad, but before I could think much about it, she put on an Elvis record and started dancing all by herself to the music. She stopped long enough to grab a pack of cigarettes off a table and offered one to me before lighting up her own. Diane and I had started smoking behind her mother's back, but I didn't start smoking all the time until we moved to Jamestown. I was afraid to do it in school at Southwestern because you would get suspended the first time you got caught, and the second time in one semester could get you expelled, so I never tried it. And you would get caught. At the new school, the girls' bathrooms were so full of smoke all the time that you could hardly see your own reflection in the mirror. The teachers must have given up trying to catch anyone.

I felt like Jackie was a little too tough for me, but there was something satisfying about being with her, so I kept right on hanging out with her. She fixed me up with some blind dates, but none of them were very nice people. Most of them drank beer and wanted me to drink, too. One night I decided to give it a try after they convinced me that I didn't know what I was missing until I tried it. It was planned that I would go to a party with a boy that Jackie knew.

Jackie's date was called Joe, and I was with a boy called Jerry. He wasn't bad looking and he even seemed to be more polite than the others she had hooked me up with, but all he talked about was getting bombed. We went to the party given by another one of the girls from Jamestown. When I walked in, I saw a bunch of kids crammed in the living room of a small apartment. There were beer bottles on every table and some on the floor. I recognized some of the kids from the skating rink in Celoron. I had no sooner walked in the room than Jerry grabbed a beer and handed it to me. "Here you go," he said, "by the looks of everyone else we've got some catching up to do."

The lights were dim in the room and as I went in further, I saw kids making out all over the place. Someone was playing records in the corner and Elvis' *Loving You* was turned up loud. I turned the bottle up to my lips and started drinking. I didn't like the taste, but I kept on anyway. The more I drank, the more I liked the other people there and pretty soon I was dancing better than I ever had before. Jerry seemed to like me more and more. One time he said, "You're someone who really ought to drink. You're a whole lot more fun now."

As some point I knew I had drunk way too much. I was vaguely aware of my head spinning and Jackie and Jerry walking me up and down the sidewalk. I said something about how pretty all the street lights were, and then I remember throwing up over and over and hearing Jerry say, "Oh, God, that's awful." My last conscious memory that night was of riding in the back seat of a car while someone held my head out the window. The cold wind felt good.

I woke up the next morning in Jackie's dirty, rumpled bed, still wearing my clothes, which was a good sign: I hadn't had them off with someone from the party last night. I had the worst headache I had ever had in my life. I recognized the feeling I was having as shame and self-hate. "Oh, God!" I thought. "I've turned into my father." I promised myself that my first drinking party would be my last. I tried to recall the events of the night before mainly to be sure that I hadn't gone all the way with someone. Later, I asked Jackie if anything like that happened and she assured me that I didn't stop throwing up long enough for anyone to give it a thought.

"One minute you were dancing with everyone, and the next you were bombed," she said grinning. "I've never seen anyone get bombed as fast as you did. You probably would have lost your cherry if you hadn't gotten sick, because you sure were acting sexy with the boys. Jerry was starting to drool."

All I wanted to do was get home and get in my own bed. It was a long walk from Jackie's to my house, but I decided to go for it and maybe my head would get better with cold fresh air. When I got there, I was amazed to find Dad acting like a father. "Where the hell have you been?" he demanded. He stood there glaring at me in the middle of the day, and on a Saturday when he should have been out drinking.

My head still ached and I guess I had been spending too much time around Jackie because I had picked up some of her attitude. I looked at him and winced because my head hurt worse when I looked up. "I've been out drinking," I said. "I thought you'd be proud of me."

"You better not be drinking at your age!" He was furious. "That girl you're hanging around with is nothing but a juvenile delinquent. I'll have you sent to reform school if you keep this up! Do you hear me?"

"Of course I hear you. You're shouting at me." I started to go up stairs and then changed my mind. "Do you know where they send people who shout at someone who's been out drinking?" I asked. "Aren't you afraid of going to the nuthouse? Oh, that's right, you're the only one who gets to send people away. And now, you're going to send me where?"

"Aw nuts!" he yelled, "I'm not going to listen to this bullshit! Just remember the next time you're going to drink underage and stay out all night, I'll call the police on you!" And with that he went out.

Dad scared me with the things he said to me. I had every reason to believe he would call the police on me, and no reason to believe he wouldn't. I stopped hanging around with Jackie and started staying close to home again. I spent my time talking on the phone to Diane when I could catch her and sometimes I would ride the bus to Celoron and go to the skating rink, or visit old friends. Mother wasn't home much during my juvenile delinquent days and I was glad she wasn't. Stopping with that gang wasn't just because I was afraid of Dad. I really didn't like the way it made me feel to be with people like that.

I didn't hear from Jackie for a long time and then one day she called me. "Hey," she said, "How're you doin'. Long time, no see. Listen, I need you to do a favor for me. My boyfriend's brother just got out of the service and I need to fix him up with someone nice like you. You know, he's five years older than the rest of us and he needs someone who acts older, so I thought of you. How about it?"

"I don't know, Jackie," I said. " I still remember that hangover from the party I went to with you. I'm not up for any more of that. Besides, I don't know anything about this guy."

"There won't be any drinking. My boyfriend doesn't like me to drink, anyway. This guy is really nice and he wants to meet a nice girl. He said he does not want to meet a slut, and that leaves out everyone else I know but you." She laughed. "Just kidding, kinda. So, how about it?"

I agreed to meet her boyfriend's brother who was just out of the service. "I've got to be home before my dad gets in, Jackie."

"No problem. Relax," she said.

XIII

Jackie's boyfriend's brother, Sherm, was handsome in an angular sort of way. He was about six feet tall and as skinny as I was, but he had nice shoulders and you could see the outline of muscles under the sleeves of his soft, suede jacket. He had nice eyes that he informed me later were hazel, not blue, and his hair was light brown. He had a nice face. I told Jackie that I wanted them to pick me up at my house for our date that night and I made sure it was cleaned up before they came. I thought it couldn't hurt for him to see that all of Jackie's friends don't live the way she does. The first thing I noticed when they came in was the way Sherm smelled. It was a combination of aftershave lotion, tobacco, cold fresh air and the suede jacket he wore. I never knew a guy could smell that good.

I was wearing a new skirt that was charcoal gray with little pink and yellow stitched designs on it and a pink sweater that I bought at Grant's Department store the day before in Jamestown. I almost called Jackie to tell her that I couldn't make it because I couldn't get my hair to look right after washing it and setting it the night before. I had used a new shampoo and it didn't work as good as the old one, but before I could decide about it, they were knocking on my door.

Jackie's boyfriend, Eddie, drove, which put me in the back seat right away with Sherm. I was very nervous. We went to Lindy's, the burger place just outside of Jamestown where everyone hung out, and had burgers, fries and milkshakes. After we ate, we went back to town to a movie and Sherm reached over for my hand soon after it started. He didn't try for anything else and he was a gentleman in every way. He didn't drink that night and he didn't argue when I told him that I wanted to get home by eleven o'clock. When he walked me to the door, he said, "I want to see you again. Jackie has already told me that you don't make out and I respect that. I would just like to spend some time getting to know you better. Okay?"

133

I was amazed that he liked me enough to say all of that and treat me as well as he did that night. "Okay," I said.

He started to leave and then turned back. "By the way," he said, "would you still go out with me if we don't tag along with the kids? Don't get me wrong, I like kids, but I don't like to spend all of my time with them." He gestured with his head towards the car where Jackie and his brother were waiting for him and grinned and winked. I never dreamed he would call me after that first date, but he did and on the very next day.

When the phone rang, I jumped up and ran to answer it with my heart pounding, hardly daring to believe it would be him. "Hey, Babe," his voice sounded sexy to me, "I can't stop thinking about you. I hope I can see you tonight; how about it?"

"Okay," I said shyly, wishing I had some cute, sexy things to say like Jackie always did with guys.

"Oh... like I said last night, if it's all right with you I'd rather not hang around with the kids. So, how about if you and I catch another movie, or just hang out downtown by ourselves tonight?"

"Okay," I said again. "What time?"

"I'll see you at seven o'clock. Now don't get mad at me if it's a little later, okay?" He had the best voice. "I'm going to have to hitch a ride so just in case it takes longer, I don't want you to get mad at me."

"Oh," I said. "You don't have a car, do you?"

"Not yet. There was any sense in having one while I was in the service, and I just haven't had a chance to find one yet, but I can see I'm going to need one so I can take my baby out."

"Oh," I said, wishing again I could stop sounding so dumb. "Then I'll see you about seven."

That night, Sherm told me everything about himself and how rough it had been on him when his mom and dad divorced when he was a small child. He had been raised for a while by a stepfather who beat him with a belt and he had a lot of bitterness towards his mother. He said that his brother Eddie and his sister, who lived in Binghamton, had been able to get along better than he did with his mother, but he was closest to the grandmother that he was staying with now.

I had never heard anyone talk the way he did that night and I found myself opening up to him. Before I knew it, I had told him the truth about where my mother was and that my father got drunk on the weekends. I told him all about Southwestern School and how I hated the Jamestown school. I told him things that I had never even told my best friend, Diane. It was a wonderful feeling to have someone to share that with, but the bad side was that I already didn't know how I would ever get along without him if he left me. I was so excited about having someone who cared about me that I couldn't go to sleep that night and he was the first thing on my mind in the morning.

He did get a car and we spent a lot of time traveling down darkened highways in the 1955 Ford; the miles slipping silently away behind us while Elvis Presley, Ricky Nelson, or Carl Perkins crooned one romantic song after another through the radio speakers. I sat next to him so close that we were both behind the steering wheel and I felt safe and loved for the first time in my life. I was terrified when I wasn't with him that the feeling would stop. There would be an uneasy gnawing in the pit of my stomach that wouldn't go away until he came back and made the rest of the world melt away. Dad could have stayed at the beer joints at the boat landing up the street every night of the week and it wouldn't have bothered me.

One day, right after I got out of bed, there was a knock on the door. When I answered it, a nicely dressed older gentleman introduced himself as Mr. Jacobs. He said he was the truancy officer for the Jamestown Public Schools and he wanted to know why I never came to school.

I surprised myself by saying, "I don't mean to disrespect you, Mr. Jacobs, but you have a terrible school after what I was used to at Southwestern. Why are there so many kids out of control?"

Mr. Jacob's gray bushy eyebrows were raised above his dark framed glasses. "I'm sorry you feel that way," he said and cleared his throat. "But you still need to come to school. It's the law that you come until you're sixteen."

"I am," I said.

"I beg your pardon?" Mr. Jacobs looked confused at first, and then said, "Oh, you are sixteen?" and he looked at the papers that were in his hand. "Well, I see you just turned sixteen, but you should think it over carefully before making a big decision such as dropping out of school."

I couldn't get over how calm I felt. "I have made up my mind. I won't be back." I even tried to sound cheerful. "Thanks for coming." I smiled at him.

Sometimes Elsmarie would catch up with me and yell at me. "I can't believe you're being so stupid with this guy! Eileen, you're only sixteen; don't throw your future away on a guy who doesn't even have a job!"

"He's looking for a job!" I yelled back. "He's got a lot of money from getting out of the service so he doesn't have to take the first thing that comes along. Did you ever think it was possible that someone would actually want to just spend time with me?"

"Yes, and I'll bet we know why he wants to spend time with you. Can't you see you're doing the same thing I did?"

My face was hot, I was so mad at her. "Well, I'm sorry to disappoint you, but we haven't even done that yet! This is great, now you and Dad can accuse me of that. That's all he talks about to me now. Maybe Sherm and I ought to go ahead and do it so you can both be right about something. And Dad really takes the cake, doesn't he? Now that I've got someone who cares about me, he's trying to come off like Robert Young on "Father Knows Best." Where was this great concern when he brought Lee Mason home one Saturday night, passed out and Lee practically chased me around the dining room table for two hours begging me to let him teach me about love?"

Elsmarie's voice became softer. "We both know that Dad's not Robert Young. Just be careful, okay?"

Even Diane wanted me to go slow with Sherm. "I just want you to have a guy who will really be good for you. You're smart and you're pretty and you deserve the best." Her voice sounded a little strange over the phone.

"Don't worry, Sherm is the best, and he told me he loves me." When she didn't say anything back, I said, "I hope you're all right. You don't sound like yourself." Again, she didn't say anything. "Diane? What's the matter?"

"I'm pregnant." After another long silence, she said, "I think I'm about three months along now and I'm going to have to tell my parents pretty soon. My dad's going to kill me."

"What does Roger say?" It was the first time I'd ever heard her sound lost.

"He thinks it's great! Of course he's got his diploma and now that he's working construction with his dad, he's making good money. He says he's ready for a family."

I couldn't help being envious of her. "So you'll be getting married and you'll have a cute little baby and Roger will build you a great house. This is good news!" I said.

For the first time I felt like I had someone, now, too, and lately he had really been trying to talk me into going all the way. "If you get pregnant, then we'll just get married," he would whisper hoarsely in my ear after we had been kissing and hugging for a long time. We had been going further than we should lately and I wasn't sure anymore how much longer I could hold him off.

Roger and Diane got married in the little chapel at the church downtown where she had always attended. Sherm and I decided to walk to the see the ceremony because it was such a nice day. On the way home he kept squeezing my hand and once he asked, "Does my baby love me as much as I love her?"

I was so happy and all I could do was nod shyly and squeeze his hand back. I hoped he was thinking the same thing that I was. I wanted, more than anything, to marry him and have our own babies.

Not quite two weeks later, Jackie and Eddie wanted to double date because they had something they wanted to tell us. We weren't surprised when they said they had to get married because Jackie was pregnant. "When is it going to be your turn?" Jackie asked. "Don't tell us you've been keeping everything all innocent with all the time you spend together." She laughed and winked and cracked her gum. "You two ought to get it over with now and we could have a double wedding."

I didn't care about having a double wedding, and neither did Sherm, but it did seem like everyone else we knew was either married, or about to get married. I was all for getting married now, especially since Sherm and I had gone all the way. I had thought that finally giving in to him would make me feel happy, but instead, I only felt guilty and ashamed. It wasn't at all what I thought it would be. It hurt and I felt embarrassed about our bodies, but it seemed to make Sherm very happy, so I guess it was worth it for that reason. "I hope you get pregnant," he would whisper to me after it was over.

I hoped so, too, because I wanted to have Sherm's baby more than anything. I could just picture us in a cute little apartment with our little baby between us. We would be such a happy family. But it didn't happen the first month, and the second month, I was late and I thought for a while I might be. Sherm got all excited and told his family before we even had a test and the next thing I knew we were picking out wedding rings at the jewelry store.

"What if it turns out I'm not pregnant?" I asked Sherm on the way home from getting our rings. I was so afraid of what his answer might be that I could hardly breathe.

"Well," he said, "if you aren't pregnant yet, then it's just a matter of time; so I think we should get married anyway." He grinned and hugged me even tighter with his right arm around me as we drove down the street towards my house. It was the middle of the day and no one was home and, for the first time, I was looking forward to what we would do when we got inside the house because I wanted to make him as happy as he made me. We didn't get to do much because I found out I wasn't pregnant after all once I got in the house. I was disappointed and I felt like Sherm was too, but he said it didn't matter. He said we could get married anyway.

Two weeks later, Sherm and I stood in front of Reverend McEntarfer at the Celoron Methodist Church. I had remembered all the important things to do. I had a new dress that I bought the day before at Lynn's Dress Discount Store; it was blue, because white was only for virgins. I had made sure that Mother got home for the wedding. We had our marriage license and had gone to see the minister just last week and he agreed to perform the ceremony. My heart sank when he said something about talking to him a few times before the wedding, but Sherm said, "We have to get married next week because that's the time I can get off work."

I did look around in church to see who was there for the wedding and was glad to see Diane had walked over from her mother's house.

Grandma Stewart sat up in the front pew looking very nice, but when she saw me, she shook her head and said, "You're too young to get married."

I was really glad to see Mother there. Dad didn't get back with her until late the night before because he had to go after work. Of course the real miracle was that he actually made it down and back on a Thursday night. Mother didn't seem to have anything to say about my wedding plans; maybe she didn't know what to say. It was probably pretty obvious to her and everyone else that I was off in my own little world and the people around me could have been nothing more than fixtures for all I cared. I wanted them all there because I had some vague idea that they should be there, but not because I had any idea as sophisticated or mature as wanting to share our special moment. The only person I needed to share anything with was the young man who was going to be my husband. It was as though I had spent my life bobbing around in the sea on nothing but a raft and Sherm was pulling me out of the swirling water into a safe, dry boat.

Regardless of the apparent lack of interest on the part of the bride and groom in the wedding congregation, we were married in front of a small gathering of family and friends. Mom was wearing a nice turquoise dress; probably something that Grandma had given her, but she looked kind of pretty. So there we all were: Sherm was wearing a suit and Dad had even dragged his old suit coat out of the closet and he was all dressed up. I thought we all looked pretty good. We stood in front of the same altar where I had given my heart to God just a few short years ago and the tears fell freely down both of our faces as we said our vows to each other. We would learn as time passed that our commitment was blessed by God and that it would last a lifetime.

Sherm's grandmother had been very tense and quiet about the whole thing, but she said she would have cake and coffee for us at her house after the ceremony. We didn't think much about what anyone said or thought because we had our own little apartment to go to at the end of the day. Getting through the reception was torture for both of us. Neither side of our families were having a good time. No one seemed to know what to say, so we all just kind of sat around and sighed. Sherm's grandfather tried to tell some corny jokes and everyone tried to laugh politely. Finally, everyone had all the cake they wanted and Sherm and I had opened the wedding gifts, which were nice, and we had thanked everyone. Before I could figure out what to do next, Sherm stood up and kind of looked around the room and said, "Well, we have to go now. Thank you for everything," and the next thing I knew he was pulling me out the door towards the car and we left laughing.

For the first time that I could remember I felt happy. Sherm and I closed ourselves up in that apartment and the rest of the world melted away. We made love all the time and he always seemed to like it the same. I didn't know how Sherm was able to go to work all day and then make love all night, but he did. As for me, I loved being held so close to him and I felt so good about being married and that we weren't committing any sins anymore.

One day, the landlord came to the door. He asked to come in and the look on his face made me kind of nervous. I guess he was embarrassed instead of nervous because his face got kind of red when he spoke, "Look here," he said, "I know you two are young and just got married, but the neighbors are tired of hearing you run bath water at all hours of the night. Now you need to cut that out. From now on, no bath water after 10:00 p.m." And having said that, he left.

I was so embarrassed that my face was bright red, but Sherm was mad about it. "I pay the rent here and we can take a bath any damn time we want to!" he said after the man had gone, but I hoped he would calm down because I loved our little apartment and I didn't want to get kicked out.

Sherm had a job at a service station just four blocks away so he was able to walk to work even though we had the car. He made enough money for us to pay our weekly rent on the apartment and buy groceries. He said, "No wife of mine is going to work!" so I stayed home and cleaned the apartment everyday. We had a small television set in the living room and after the cleaning was done, I watched some of the stories. I didn't know if our life was normal because I didn't know what normal was. I wish I could say that I reached out to my mother during that time, but the truth is that I didn't give her much thought. We each had so little self-esteem that no one in our little family had anything to give one another. Each one of us was an empty well by that time trying to find someone, or something to fill the void. I had found someone that I thought would surely make everything all right.

XIV

Being married to Sherm meant that I could leave all of the bad things from my childhood behind. I never asked him if we could go see Dad and I was used to not seeing Mother, so it seemed right to just concentrate on being married. I wanted to start a family so badly that I had begun to think about it all the time. Jackie was almost ready to have her baby and sometimes she and Eddie would come to visit us, and I had to fight back tears after she would tell me how great it was to feel the baby moving around inside of her. Diane was about at the same stage with her pregnancy, and Elsmarie was expecting again with her new husband George. It seemed like everyone was having babies except me so I still felt different.

Elsmarie, by the way, had been very mad at me for a long time because she said that since I met Sherm I didn't care about her, or anyone else anymore. I never thought I'd be able to say that I didn't care what anyone thought about me, but the truth was that as long as Sherm was happy with me, I didn't need anyone else. Sherm preferred to spend time alone with me, too. I also did not want to be around anyone who said bad things about him and Elsmarie had said quite a few things about him. We had gotten into some arguments about Sherm.

"Well, you two can't just shut out the world, you know. Someday you're going to need somebody and there won't be anyone there for you because of the way you've treated people," she said. "How do you think Dad feels? He said you treat him like he's not even there."

"I just can't get over how you take up for Dad, now. I can remember being left alone by him when I was six years old and, after you married Rodney, I might as well have been living alone from Thursday through to Sunday, and I was ten years old!" I just shook my head when I looked at her, "Now I'm supposed to feel bad for him because I'm paying attention to Sherm instead of him? Well, I don't feel bad for him." I didn't want to say it to her, but I think she was just jealous. Why couldn't she understand that we were on our honeymoon and that's why we wanted to be alone? The only time Elsmarie and I teamed up together after I got married was on Thanksgiving that year. Sherm and I had moved from the apartment to a little house and we had agreed that the dinner would be held at our house because there was more room. Elsmarie and George had a small apartment and Dad had also moved to a place just big enough for him, and Mother. Elsmarie did the turkey and she and her family came early in the day so we could get everything set up. Dad had gone to get Mother the Sunday before and when I talked with her on the phone, she said they would be over as soon as Dad got back from the store.

The house smelled like the roast turkey and pumpkin pie that was in the oven and the stove top was covered with cooking pots. We had potatoes and squash and cranberry sauce, and a tray of dinner rolls was on the small counter top waiting to be popped into the oven as soon as the turkey came out. Sherm was sound asleep on the couch and George was expected back from deer hunting as soon as the sun went down. Peggy, at three, pretended to read a story from a book she held on her lap to her new little brother, Kevin, who was almost asleep in the playpen. Elsmarie and I were getting along better than we had in a long time. We joked about cooking together just like the way we had seen the old aunts doing it when we were kids and then realized that someday we would be the old aunts. I pretended to be Aunt Mildred when little Peggy asked for a cookie. I raised my eyebrows and pursed my lips together and waited for the sweet little child to go back in the other room and then I said, using an Aunt Mildred tone, "I gave her one cookie, but I can't give her another. She has to learn that cookies cost money."

"Well, what can you expect?" Elsmarie said, using her best Aunt Mildred facial expression and tone of voice. "Look at who her mother is and it's no wonder the child doesn't know about such things."

"Speaking of Mother," I said in a more serious tone, "where are they? It's after four o'clock."

"Well, I'll give you three guesses where dear old Dad is," said

Elsmarie. "You know what? Let's just go get Mother and bring her over here and we'll have a nice Thanksgiving without him. I'll call her," she said. She went into the living room to the phone and I could hear her end of the conversation, "Is he home, yet, Mother?" There was a long pause while she listened. "Well, Mother, there's no sense in you sitting there alone on Thanksgiving. I'm coming over to pick you up," and then, "now, Mother, don't be silly, he might not be home until midnight. No, I'm coming over to pick you up. We've got dinner ready here." Then I heard her say, "Okay, fine, then sit there. We're going to eat!" I could hear her slam the phone down.

"Can you believe that?" she said as she came into the kitchen. "I give up!" She lit another cigarette, even though she had just put one out. "Well, the hell with it! We'll wait until dark and then George will be here and we'll just eat. We're going to have a good day without them. We sure know how to have holidays without them, don't we?" And then she stopped sounding quite so mad. "At least we have food, you and I can both remember holidays with no food."

Elsmarie poured us each another cup of coffee and said, "How can she keep on loving him after all he's done to her?" She looked thoughtful for a while and then she said in a very soft voice, "Eileen, do you remember that Christmas when we lived down on Second Street and Dad never came home?"

"I remember a lot of times that Dad never came home," I said.

"Yeah, me too, but I'm talking about the year that we got those two little rubber dolls and that set of wooden blocks; Ma said that Santa Claus brought them." She sighed and said, "I'll never get over that. You were just a little kid, but I was almost ten and I watched her go across the street on Christmas Eve to that little store and she charged those things for us. If she hadn't done that, we wouldn't have anything that year."

"I never knew that," I said. "I never thought about it after. You know, about how she got those things. How did you know she charged them?"

"Because I asked her when she got back. I knew she didn't have any money, so I asked her. She didn't want to tell me, but I kept asking. Finally, she said, 'The man said I could pay later, when your father gets home.' She was mad because I kept asking." Elsmarie

144

sighed again and then stood up. "Let's get dinner on the table so we can eat when George gets here, and maybe we can take something over to Ma later."

Elsmarie and I didn't often share moments like we did that Thanksgiving. She was always criticizing me for not standing up to Sherm, but she never stood up to George. He was definitely the boss in their house. She was just as busy as I was getting his laundry done and his breakfast and supper on the table on time. Oh, and she also had to pack George's lunch pail every morning. I didn't have to pack Sherm's lunch anymore because he had a different job and now he ate his lunch out. He worked long hours and sometimes I wished I could go somewhere during the day, but he said that wouldn't be right for me to be off having fun while he was working, and besides, he never knew for sure when he was getting home and I needed to be there to get his supper when he came in.

We moved again to a better place and Sherm had a new job with regular work hours. It paid more money than any of the other ones he'd had before and we were able to buy a nice used car that was only four years old. On Friday afternoons, when he came home from work, I would be all ready to go and he would take a quick shower and put on clean clothes and we'd take off for the night. We never knew where we were going until we got there. I couldn't imagine two people being closer. Sherm would have his arm tight around me holding me close and if the car had to be shifted I would do it with my right hand slipping the gear in perfectly as he pushed in the clutch. It was as though everything that needed to be said was just understood between us and we never had to talk during those long drives.

One night, early that spring, we went to bed and I was bothered by a dream that seemed to go on for a very long time. It was very confusing, but very real and Dad and Elsmarie and Mother were all in it. In this dream something horrible was happening to one of us, but I couldn't discover who it was. All of a sudden I knew something horrible was happening to Mother. I remember trying to scream, "No!" and then I woke up with a start. It was so real I was crying. I sat up and woke Sherm. "We've got to get my mother out of that hospital!" I was sobbing so hard I could barely get the words out.

145

"Okay," he said, holding me. "Come on, now... shh. Stop crying." He tried to comfort me.

"I mean it!" I said. "If Dad doesn't want to do it, then we have to. We can't leave her there anymore." I couldn't sleep the rest of the night. Part of the time I was up sitting in the kitchen drinking coffee and waiting for morning so I could talk to Elsmarie and Dad about getting Mother out of the hospital. It was Saturday, so Dad would be home. He had calmed down a lot with his drinking and the past few times that I saw him he seemed to be lonesome. Maybe the time would be right for everyone now.

I called Elsmarie as soon as the sun was up and it turned out that she had been having strong feelings about getting Mother out, too. We decided to go together to see Dad. I told her I'd pick her up.

Dad looked surprised to see both of his daughters standing on his doorstep. He had moved again, this time to a house. It happened that it was the same house that they moved to right after they lost the house on Oak Street. It was, in fact, the house that they were living in when I was born. It was a small two-story place with just two rooms downstairs and a short stairway in the living room that led to the two bedrooms and the bathroom upstairs. It wasn't as shabby as the house in Celoron, but it wasn't as nice as the duplex on Eighth Street. It just looked the way places look when the landlord doesn't want to spend any money on them; the pattern on the linoleum was worn away in spots and the furniture consisted of some mismatched pieces from the second-hand store. "Come in," Dad said, stepping aside. He had been sitting at the kitchen table. "I just made coffee."

Elsmarie got cups out for us, Dad poured the coffee and I got the milk out of the refrigerator and when the three of us were seated at the table, Elsmarie looked at me and said, "You start."

"I had a horrible dream about Mother the other night, Dad. The dream was so confusing that I don't even know what happened in it, but something bad was happening to her and it made me realize that she's been down there all the years and except for visits, that's been her home. We all just go on with our lives like we don't care about her." I stopped and looked away for a minute. "Elsmarie and I have talked and we want her out of there for good." I looked at my sister.

Elsmarie picked up on it, "We think she would rather be with you, but if you don't want to take her, then Eileen and I are going to figure out how to talk her into spending part of the time with her and part of it with me."

"I know she's been there too long," Dad said. "I'll get her out. I want her to come home, too. It bothers me that she's been there so long."

Elsmarie said, "If she comes home, you can't get drunk all the time. You can't expect her to live like that."

"I know. I know." He sounded mad, but he looked guilty, and then said, "I'll get her out and I'm not going to drink anymore." He got up from the table and walked over to the window, but I thought I saw his eyes turn red and watery just before he turned his back.

"Okay," I said. "When are you going to call and arrange it? I don't want you to do this next week, or next month. I mean now, Dad," and then, realizing that it was Saturday, "Monday. You should call on Monday."

"I will. I'll call on Monday and I'll get her as soon as they say that I can. She'll probably have to come home for a thirty-day trial period before I can sign the release. Dad kept his word and Mother came home the following Saturday for her thirty-day trial visit.

XV

Of course there must be rules for everything. The discharge rule at the State Hospital at Helmuth was that a patient must have a thirty-day home trial before final discharge. I knew there were thirty-day home trial periods that were extended for vacuum cleaners and certain other appliances, but I'm not sure what the reasoning was behind this. You didn't need a thirty-day trial before any other hospital discharge. No one said, "Take the baby home for thirty days and see how it works out, and if you don't like it, then bring it back." What could possibly be proven in thirty days? Was the patient supposed to "go crazy" again within that time period and if he or she didn't, then he must be okay for good? Mother had been down there for approximately fourteen years, only leaving when she was on home visits. During her stay, she had paid her way with the sweat of her brow while working at the hospital laundry and she had endured countless indignities, from the loss of her right to privacy to her loss of freedom. What could they think they could possibly have gained from thirty more days? The answer is simple; it was the rule.

The thirty days of Mother's pre-release home trial was like nothing I had ever experienced. My parents showed up together at my apartment and sat at the kitchen table for coffee and conversation. There were no arguments. I invited them for supper one Friday and Mother showed up early. She had walked up from their house on Maple Street. "Mom, how come you didn't tell me you were coming? I always have the car on Fridays, I could have picked you up."

"I don't mind walking," she said. "I came to help you with supper." She was wearing a light cotton print dress, her hair was curled, and she wore a touch of lipstick. "I told your father that I would be here so he's coming straight from work. It's okay if I stay, isn't it?"

"Of course it is, Mom," I said. I felt bad that she felt she had to ask my permission.

"Have you got something I can do for you?" she asked.

"You can sit down and have some coffee," I said. "Oh, I know what you can do, if you will." I looked at her hopefully. "Will you show me how to make pie crust? I just can't do it the way you do. Mine is either so tough that you have to chop it in pieces in order to eat it, or it's so flaky that you can't get it out of the pie pan without it crumbling."

"Sure," she said. As soon as I got out the ingredients, she measured them into a bowl. "The trick is to cut your shortening into the flour until it all looks like little navy peas before you add your water." I noticed how capable her hands were as she worked the dough. When she had it all mixed, she said, "Now you try rolling it out." She looked up and our eyes met for a moment and in that instant we shared what we should have had always. We had experienced it fleetingly before; it was there that time on Main Street when Mom refused to take my gloves to warm her hands that were red with cold as the snow swirled around us in the blustery wind; and it was there on more than one occasion when she said, "Sit down and eat, now," and I knew she was giving me the last slice of bread in the house. In those steady looks, her eyes said, "I am your mother and I will take care of you," and for a brief instant I was not the sassy, mean little kid, nor the self-absorbed, bossy teenager, I was simply her child.

"Thanks, Mom." I opened my mouth, wanting to say something meaningful to her, but nothing came out. I wanted to throw my arms around her and tell her and how much I had missed her and how sorry I was for being such a miserable daughter over the years, but instead I tried rolling out the dough. "How's this, Mom?" I asked, surprised at how small my own voice sounded. The moment passed.

May 25th was Mom's birthday and Elsmarie and I had talked about doing something special for her. One of the things that she loved when she was home was listening to the Breakfast Club on the radio. Every morning, the Breakfast Club was held on the top floor of Bigelows Department Store. Bigelows was the finest department store in all of Jamestown. We used to make fun of both Grandma

Stewart and Mom because every time they knew something was bought there they would say, "You know, it came from Bigelows," but they never said the name out loud; They would say everything right out until it came to the name, Bigelows. And then they would whisper the name almost like it had something to do with church. Anyway, the Breakfast Club was one of the main programs offered by the radio station that was broadcast from the top floor of Jamestown's famous department store. People having birthdays would get special recognition and a gift from Bigelows just by attending. We invited Grandma Stewart to join us and decided to take Peggy and the four of us went to the event on the morning of Mom's birthday.

Grandma was wearing her dark blue coat and matching hat and her white hair curled softly around her face. When I was little I thought she looked fluffy because she was kind of plump and dimpled with round cheeks. Mom tried to hide how excited she was that morning. When we picked her up, she said she'd been up for hours. Her face was slightly flushed with excitement and she looked really pretty.

I guess we were all a little nervous as we got off the elevator in Bigelows on the top floor. The tables had white linen cloths and little centerpieces. The food was good and when the announcer came and interviewed Mom, she was nervous, but she spoke right into his microphone and told him that we were four generations at the table. She went on and introduced all of us and then he said, "We aren't supposed to ask a lady her age, Mrs. Sandquist, but you can tell it if you want to." He held the microphone out for her to speak.

"I'm fifty years old today," she said.

"Well, you don't look to be that old. You are fifty years young."

"Thank you," she said. "I feel that everything is going good now and I hope it doesn't start going the other way."

I thought that announcer was right when he said that about Mom. She did look good and when she got this thirty-day thing over, Dad said he would take her to a dentist so she could get a partial plate where those two teeth were missing because she was very self-conscious about it. Every time she smiled she still put her tongue there.

Dad kept his word about not drinking as far as I could tell. I know that they went to see Elsmarie and George some of the time and once they invited all of us to their house and they both cooked supper for us. When we got there, Mom looked at me and said, "Can you imagine it? We brought you home to this very house after you were born."

It was hard to imagine and, looking at all of us together right then, it was even harder to imagine that it hadn't always been that way. Sherm and George were in the living room keeping the kids occupied while Elsmarie and I set the table for Mom and Dad while they tended to things over at the stove. The meal was good and there was soft conversation and jokes around the table. Afterwards, Elsmarie and Mom and I cleaned up and did all the dishes together. The house seemed bright and pretty and homey and not just some furnished place they were renting. Maybe it was the hope and the love that filled the room, or the little touches that Mom managed to add when she was home. Her old cotton tablecloth that had been around for years had been ironed until the creases were sharp and the house was clean and smelled like supper.

The idea that it could have always been this way for our family if we had all cooperated long ago was so overwhelming that I couldn't think about it. What could anyone do with that notion at that point? Could it be that all the years of frustration, longing and fantasizing were for nothing? I couldn't allow myself to consider that for longer than a second without wanting to yell, curse and do something physically violent to someone; but who? When it came to deciding responsibility, I had to ask myself why I didn't come to my conclusion that she needed to be home much earlier.

We wanted the thirty days to go fast so she could get that last trip to the hospital over with and she could finally be out for good. Before long, the month was up and Dad was taking Mom back on Saturday and she would be back the following Friday. The Thursday evening before they left, I was going to the laundromat to do the clothes and they came by as I was getting ready to leave and offered to go along. Sherm was helping his brother fix a car and I really was glad for the company.

When we got there, Dad and Mom helped carry the baskets of

laundry in while I stuffed clothes into washers and loaded the quarters into the slots to get them started. Mom helped measure soap and checked them all to make sure they were going good and then we decided to sit outside on the bench in front while waiting for the wash to finish. It was a beautiful summer evening and the sun was just beginning to set. It happened that I ended up sitting between my parents and we just sat there without talking and watched a beautiful sunset together. Sitting there between them felt strangely familiar and safe. I knew I had been there before, but I just couldn't remember when. It had to be when I was a small child, way before all of the bad things started happening. A time when Carl and Irene shared as parents to make the child safe that they had brought into this world together. I knew I was experiencing a part of my parents' history at that moment.

Dad and Mom stopped by on Saturday morning to say goodbye to us before leaving for the hospital. Mom was wearing a pretty black and white checked dress. Her hair looked nice and she was wearing a little makeup. Sherm said, "Ma, you look pretty!"

She said, "Oh, go on!" She shook her head and she tried to look annoyed at him, but she was really pleased and couldn't hide her smile.

"You do look pretty," I said, "Well, this is the last trip back for you and then you're home for good."

"I guess I'll be back Friday," she said, looking at Dad who was nodding in agreement. "Your father said we're going to go look at new house trailers when I get back." She looked at him again and smiled. "I guess we might as well go so we can get this last trip over."

I got up and gave Mom a kiss and she hugged me for a minute before going out the door. I said goodbye to Dad and stood at the top of the stairs and watched them get into the car and drive off. I thought about talking to Elsmarie about a family celebration dinner for Sunday. Sometimes time seemed to stand still for me. We had been married two years and Sherm and I still didn't have a baby on the way, but we had agreed to look into adoption if something didn't happen soon. I told him that I might as well go to work seeing as we didn't have children, but he still said that "no wife of his was going to work." The little apartment we lived in was really pretty nice. There were four large sunny rooms and all but the kitchen had hardwood floors that had been kept polished so they showed very little signs of wear. The rooms were large and sunny with tall windows and there were two porches, one off the bedroom and the other off the living room with railings around them that were high and strong. It would be a good place to bring a baby.

The other nice thing about the apartment was that we were just three blocks away from Mom's youngest brother and his wife. I had never really known Aunt Tina before this move. She was just someone who was in the photograph with Uncle Dick at Grandma Stewart's house. He was handsome in a white sailor uniform and his hair, the same dark brown as Mom's, showed underneath his sailor cap and it grew in crisp curls even though his hair was short. Elsmarie said she was always in love with Uncle Dick when she was a little girl. Aunt Tina was slim and pretty in the picture with shoulder length hair that curled under softly. The first thing I noticed when I visited Aunt Tina was that she had the same photograph, but in a larger size. "Grandma has the same picture," I said.

"That's our wedding picture," she laughed, "I was always surprised she kept that out. You know she wasn't very happy when we got married." Aunt Tina laughed a lot and she loved to talk. I knew that they had been married about fourteen years and that Aunt Tina had had about five miscarriages before they adopted their little girl who was napping in the next room.

"Why not?" I asked, still looking at the young couple in the photograph.

"Because I'm Italian." she said.

"So what?" I answered. I was really being polite because I did know that Swedish people didn't like Italians. Dad had told me that he never wanted to catch me out with an Italian boy. When I asked him why, he said they all had greasy hair, black leather jackets, rode motorcycles and couldn't be trusted.

"Oh, she almost disowned your uncle! But she came around after a while so it's all right now." Aunt Tina was very short and had gotten a little plump over the years, but she looked good. She had a dark complexion and big brown eyes that seemed to sparkle with fun, but the best thing was her smile and the way she always made everyone feel good. You never felt like you were going to be a bother when you knocked on her door.

I visited her often while we lived on Main Street. As soon as my housework was done, I'd head down the block and around the corner. If Sherm came home early for some reason he couldn't get mad at me for going off and leaving the house in a mess so I could relax. Aunt Tina and Uncle Dick lived upstairs in a big wooden shingled house and her father and a bachelor brother lived downstairs. Their apartment was beautiful, and spotless. They had pretty living room furniture that was deep and comfortable and made you feel like you could take a nap when you sat on it. The furniture was a very pale shade of rose and there were print throw pillows scattered around on the couch and matching chair and on Uncle Dick's recliner. She crocheted beautiful Afghans and they were on the backs of the furniture so you could just reach around and cover up with something on chilly days. Family photographs in elegant silver frames along with pretty glass figurines were placed on the polished wooden tables. "Your house is really pretty," I told her the first time I visited.

"Well, we've saved our money so we could buy nice things, and then if you take good care of them they last a long time. Most of the things here we've had a long time."

We usually sat in her kitchen for my visits drinking coffee. Or, I should say, I sat and she seemed to always be cooking or washing something at the sink as she talked. "You'll see. You'll be able to get nice things too. You just have to be patient. You two are just babies yet." She had a way of being able to say anything without sounding mean. For one thing, she smiled all the time and she acted like she really cared about you. She would always ask, "Have you eaten lunch yet?"

I would always answer, "I'm not hungry, Aunt Tina, I don't usually eat lunch anyway."

That would send her straight to the refrigerator saying, "Let me see... I don't have anything in here to eat... well, here's a little lunch meat and some cheese." She would keep bringing things out until the table was full of several different kinds of lunch meat and cheeses and sandwich spreads and pickles and then she'd say, "You should have a little something with a sandwich," and then the covered dishes would come out and by the time she finished "putting out a little something," she would look up and say, "Just have a little sandwich. You're too skinny anyway," and then she might flash a mischievous grin and say, "If you two kids want to make a baby, you've got to be strong, you know it takes more than just doing it all the time."

When she said things like that, my face would get red and that would just make her laugh more. "Look at you blush, that's so cute. It's all right, we were young once. We used to do it all the time, too." She laughed again, "Sometimes we still do, but usually Uncle Dick· falls asleep on the couch before I get a chance to kiss him good night. But he's a good guy. I wouldn't trade him."

When I told Aunt Tina about getting Mom out of the hospital, she said, "I'm so glad to hear you say that. I told your Uncle Dick that she shouldn't ever have been put down there, away from her children. I mean it, I always liked Irene." She put her dish towel down and sat down at her kitchen table opposite me. "Your mother was the only one in the family who was nice to me when your Uncle and I got married." She shook her head slowly. "I've just thought it was such a shame that she had to stay down there while your father..." Aunt Tina interrupted herself, and then went on, "Listen, I don't mean any harm to your father and I probably shouldn't say anything, but..." She lowered her voice. "I think your father's drinking has something to do with him keeping her down there. I mean, what was so wrong with her? I never could see what was so wrong with her."

"I know, Aunt Tina, it's been awful for years. I just couldn't figure out what to do..."

"You? You couldn't do anything!" she said loudly. "You and your sister were just children!" she said, getting up again. "What could you do? You couldn't tell the adults what to do, but your father... well, he should be glad to have her home now. He's all alone since you got married. Who does he have? I'm not surprised he wants her home now." She shook her head again slowly and said, "I know I should shut my mouth, but I don't see where your father's family has ever tried to do anything for Irene, but they talk like they know so much about her. Your Aunt Mildred has seen Grandma downtown before and she's made it sound to her like your mother was some kind of hopeless case, or something… I wondered how she would know anyway, have they ever gone down to see Irene?"

"Not that I know of. I think the only place they would have seen her is at Ladies Aid. Mom always liked to go to the Salvation Army for Ladies Aid," I said.

"Well, I admit we didn't go to see her often, but we went a couple of times and it was so awful to see her there I told your Uncle Dick we should wait until she's home to visit her." Aunt Tina looked sad. "And you know, with all the troubles we had, you know, for years I was either pregnant and had to stay in bed to try to keep it, or I had just lost a baby…" her voice trailed off.

"You've been through a lot, Aunt Tina," I said.

"Well, you said she's coming home Friday? I'm going to tell Dick that we should go see her and tell her that I'm happy for her," and then she said, "Oh, wait, maybe you're going to all get together. We can come another time."

"No, you go. I'm going Saturday. I'm not sure what time they'll get back, so Sherm and I will probably still go out Friday night like we usually do and then we'll go Saturday," I told her. "You go see her on Friday. She likes you and she'd be glad to see you. I'm going to talk to Elsmarie about having some kind of celebration on Sunday."

XVI

It was Saturday morning. The Saturday morning that I was going to
visit my mother who was, after fourteen years, no longer a patient at
the State Mental Hospital at Helmuth, NY. I was in the bathroom
combing my hair before going when I heard the phone ring. Sherm
was out in the living room and I knew he'd get it. A moment later,
Sherm came in the bathroom and I looked at the expression on his
face in his reflection in the mirror and I knew something horrible had
happened. "Honey," he said softly, "I want you to come out here in
the kitchen and sit down."

"Why?" I said, still looking at his reflection rather than turning
to face him.

He started to put his hands on my shoulders to turn me around
and I spun around and out of his grasp. "What? Tell me what's
wrong!" I looked into his eyes and he looked away. There was a long
silence during which I held my breath and watched the muscle in
Sherm's jaw move and read the compassion in his eyes. The
bathroom light buzzed softly.

"That was your dad on the phone. We've got to go right now.
He's in pretty bad shape, Hon." Sherm looked at the floor and then
he pulled me towards him so my head was tight against his chest.
"Your mother is dead," he said.

"No!" I screamed. I jerked away from him. He kept trying to put
his arms around me, but I twisted away. "Why are you saying that?
You heard it wrong! It can't be my mother, she just came home!
Can't you see I'm almost ready to go see her?" I looked at his face
for some sign that he was trying to pull me in on some horrible joke,
but he couldn't look at me. "Okay," I said, "maybe somebody died…
please say it isn't my mother!"

Sherm managed to get me into his arms and held me tightly as I
gave in momentarily to this nightmare and my mind and body

157

returned to a state that was all too familiar. Everything in me turned off. Someone would tell me what to do next; maybe Sherm could tell me. "We've got to go to your father, Honey. He's all alone there." Sherm took the comb from my hand and laid it down gently on the side of the porcelain sink. He put his arm around me and held me close to him all the way down the stairs and put me in the car. There wasn't a sound in the car as we drove to the little house on Maple Street. Dad was waiting outside for us. He looked the same with his white shirt open at the collar and his sleeves rolled up, but his eyes were red from crying and his face was distorted with pain. He walked over to Sherm's side of the car and looked in at us.

"I'm glad you're here," he said. "They haven't come to get her yet."

When he said that, I got out and started to walk towards the house. Dad came right up behind me and said, "Don't go look at her. You don't want to see her like that." Tears started running down his cheeks again and his nose was running. I wished I had a hanky to give him.

I didn't want to see her, but if I was supposed to, then I'd have to do that. "What happened?" I didn't know if I was crying, too, but I thought I should be, I guess it didn't matter.

"I called the ambulance and they asked me some questions and then they said they would send the doctor. He came and he said it was a stroke, or a cerebral haemorrhage... I don't know... She woke up with a headache this morning, so I gave her some aspirin and she stayed in bed. I had to go to work for a couple of hours. When I got home, she said she wasn't feeling any better so I asked her if she would try to eat some soup if I fixed it. When I brought it up just a few minutes later, she was gone."

Elsmarie came and Dad had to repeat everything he'd just told us. I listened again as though I was hearing it for the first time. We all stayed outside until the hearse arrived from Henderson-Lincoln Funeral Home. Dad said that the doctor who pronounced her dead also made the call to have her picked up. "I couldn't think," Dad said. "I hope Henderson-Lincoln was all right to call." I looked away as two men wheeled a covered body out to the waiting hearse. We stood and watched them pull away as neighbors looked out their windows at us. We all stood outside for a few minutes not talking and then Dad said, "I don't want to go back in there," meaning into the house. I shook my head; I knew I wasn't going in.

Elsmarie said, "Come on. Let's go to my house. I'll put some coffee on so we can talk. We've got to figure out what to do next."

Someone came up with ideas about what had to be done. Sherm seemed to be talking, or it might have been George, about arrangements. It never occurred to me before to wonder how funerals were planned. I had been to plenty of them over the years and I didn't think about that part. I never thought about how the immediate family members felt when they were making the arrangements. I always saw them during the visitation hours, or at the funeral itself where everyone shows up all dressed up in nice-looking dress clothes with hairdos and makeup. In fact, most of the funerals were for very elderly relatives and their family members would greet visitors with big smiles and they'd pump your hand with warm handshakes and say things like, "Doesn't she look wonderful?" or, "She's sleeping peacefully now." And sometimes nothing was said at all about the departed. I've been to funerals where people talked about everything but the loved one laying in the casket. Did those soft-spoken, cheerful acting people show up at the funeral home shortly after the death the way Dad, Elsmarie and I did? Were their complexions chalk-white with deep black circles under their eyes, and was their hair mashed down in places where a husband had tried to provide comfort by holding his young wife close to his chest? Maybe.

Mr. Henderson, or maybe it was Mr. Lincoln, met us at the door and welcomed us inside. It was a beautiful place; it might have been an elegant hotel for very rich people. The room we entered from the door was huge with very high ceilings. We were in the foyer and there were several other rooms that opened from there. The carpet was deep and the color of slate and the covering on the wall looked like silk and the woodwork around the doorways was very wide with carvings and painted a silky white. The man was very tall with carefully combed wavy white hair. He wore a dark suit that might have been black or very dark blue. After telling us how very sorry he was for our loss, he invited us into an office that was larger than my

159

living room. He asked many questions and wrote things down as we spoke.

Finally, he asked if we would like to look at clothing selections for Mother there, or would we be bringing something in that she was particularly fond of? Elsmarie and I looked at one another, each of us mentally surveying Mom's wardrobe, and then my sister said, "We'd like to look at your selections." We chose a blue dress from a glass case and described the way we'd like her hair fixed.

We answered questions for the obituary and discussed cemetery plots and learned that water-tight vaults would preserve our mother's body much longer than if we didn't have one. I controlled my impulse to ask why we would want to preserve her for a lengthy period of time because it would certainly have not been appropriate. We had to decide on family visitation times and who would be included in the family car for the funeral procession. We were advised to select pallbearers and informed that our mother would be ready for viewing at noon the next day. Then we were invited to follow the very cordial gentleman downstairs into the basement, which had also been carpeted and had the same wallpaper. It never occurred to me to wonder how people picked out caskets. I had been to lots of funerals in my time, that were mainly for aunts and uncles, and, of course, little Deborah's and Farmor's funerals, so I had seen caskets before, but I never dreamed how many there were to choose from. There were more caskets in Henderson-Lincoln's basement than I would have tried to count. There was no life insurance on Mom, so Dad settled on something that was definitely not welfare, but also didn't come with any guarantee against seepage. Dad said, "I thought they were buried in concrete vaults, anyway."

Elsmarie and I left Dad with our husbands and her children at her house while we went to shop for some decent funeral attire. Within an hour, I had picked out a black two-piece dress with a short top that zipped in the back and a pleated skirt and another one that was also black and woven, almost like linen with a straight skirt. We dragged our husbands' suits out of the backs of the closets and had Sherm go find Dad's and find a dry cleaner who would do them for us that afternoon because of our special circumstances.

I know that there was no way to have prepared for seeing Mom in her casket, but it was such a shock that I couldn't breathe at first. The room started to spin and I was glad that Sherm was holding me because I might have fallen down. Elsmarie was standing on the other side of me saying, "Oh, no," in a voice that sounded more like a whimper.

I couldn't stop staring into the casket. The woman lying there was beautiful. The blue dress was a perfect color for her and her gray-tinged chestnut hair had been arranged in soft curls all around her face. She looked like she could just open her eyes any minute, but she was still, and when I touched her hand, it was cold and hard. The baskets of flowers we had ordered had arrived and had been placed on pedestals each side of the casket. Each one had a white satin ribbon that said, "Mother," and Dad's spray of red roses was placed on the closed half of the casket. People came that I hadn't seen in years. They would walk over to the casket and look in and then come over to speak to us. Some just said, "I'm so sorry," and left. Others wanted to comment on her hair, her dress, or even ask how she died. I let everyone else do the talking. I didn't want to talk.

Uncle Dick and Aunt Tina kept wiping their eyes. She tried to smile through her tears, "I saw her the night before she died," she said. "Remember, Eileen, I told you we might go see her? Well, we took a chance and went late in the afternoon, right after Dick came home from work." Aunt Tina was always very energetic when she spoke. "I'm so glad we did, huh, Hon." She looked over at her husband whose face was full of pain over the loss of his big sister. "She looked great! I wish you could have seen her. I don't know when I've seen Irene look that happy... oh, and you should have seen her and your dad holding hands like a couple of kids."

"I saw her, too," Elsmarie said, "They came over to see us. They said they'd been looking at house trailers and they were going to the drive-in movie." Tears were running freely down Elsmarie's face.

"Didn't she look good to you?" Aunt Tina asked.

Elsmarie nodded. "She looked great. I was teasing her and I told her I hoped I didn't end up with a baby brother or sister, as good as she looked." She looked over at me, "She went to your house, too, Eileen, but you weren't home."

Aunt Sylvia and Greta came over to us. "Oh, my poor baby

brother." Aunt Sylvia's eyes were wet with tears. "It's finally over, isn't it? You and me… we've been through so much, haven't we, Cullah? When does all the trouble end, huh?"

Greta's voice had gotten deeper over the years and she sounded more like her mother, "I don't think it ever does end," she said. "It never has for us." She looked over at Elsmarie and me. "Oh, you poor things. I know this is hard on you." And then she saw Grandma and leaned down close to her and spoke in a loud voice, "I'm sorry for the loss of your daughter."

I saw Grandma try to move away, "Thank you for coming," she said. Grandma was not hard of hearing.

Cousin Joyce showed up with her older sister, Delores. They came right over to Elsmarie and me. Joyce had her arms outstretched and a pitying look on her face. She hugged me and then Elsmarie. "You poor things. We know just what you're going through, you know, we lost our mother, too, so we know just how you feel." I remembered Aunt Mildred's funeral a few years back. "Well, Uncle Carl, you did everything you could for her. She's at peace now." Cousin Joyce hugged Dad, and said, "God Bless you, you'll be in our prayers and you know if there's anything we can do, all you have to do is call." She stood with her head tilted to the side and never lost her pitying expression. "Delores and I believe that we should try to help the best we can to stand in for Mother now that she's no longer with us."

At the funeral, two of the cousins from Dad's side of the family sang *The Old Rugged Cross*, which was one of Mom's favorite hymns. We had decided that seeing as she had enjoyed the Salvation Army and had attended services whenever she could get there that it would be her wish to have the captain from the Salvation Army give the service. Dad asked his sister, Aunt Anna, to ask the Captain to officiate at the funeral. He arrived promptly and began his service as soon as the cousins finished singing. I sat in the front pew, with Dad in the middle, Elsmarie and I were on either side of him and our husbands sat next to us. The captain had been the pastor at the Salvation Army for several years. He wore the customary dark blue uniform with the dark red trim on the shoulders of his jacket and sides of his trousers. His blond hair had become very thin, leaving only wisps on the top. He began discussing the importance of being ready to go to God and went on some about what was necessary for our entry into Heaven when our time came. Having been to several funerals for Salvation Army members, I knew it was not unusual for the captain to give a rather lengthy sermon, but I couldn't help wondering when he was going to say saying something comforting about Mom. After what seemed to be a very long time, the captain said, "We don't know if Irene was a Christian. We can only hope that her soul was saved and that the Almighty God will allow her into the Kingdom of Heaven."

His words felt like stones to me. I heard Dad mumble something, but I couldn't make out what he said and I looked over at Elsmarie who was crying, but she looked really mad. The service was over shortly from that point and, thankfully, we were led out to the family car first.

"That pompous bastard!" Elsmarie spoke up as soon as the door was closed on the car. "How could he say that about Mom? He didn't bother to find out one thing about her from us."

"I figured Anna would talk to him. She knows that Irene used to walk down to Ladies Aid no matter how bad the weather was when she was home." Dad was crying again. I had never seen him cry as much as he had since Mom died. "I guess I should have gotten somebody else."

"No! You did the right thing. Mom loved the Salvation Army, more than the rest of us did." She took long drags on the cigarette. "You did the right thing, Dad. The captain did the wrong thing and I'm going to let him know it."

At the cemetery, I didn't look at the captain as he said the brief service at the grave site and I really didn't hear what he said. Pretty soon, people started walking, so I figured out that the service was over. Aunt Anna came over to where we were standing and said in her pleasant husky voice, "Carl, I've told everyone to come over to the house for coffee, I hope that's all right. You'll all come and have something, won't you?"

When we arrived at Aunt Anna's house, we saw all of the people who had been at the funeral. I looked for a place to sit outside on the lawn. I walked by Aunt Sylvia and Greta who were talking to another one of the cousins. I could hear Greta telling about the hard times they were having and that Stig owed her thousands in back child support for her daughter, Brenda. It seemed very strange that she had just graduated from high school and she was my age. I felt very old.

I saw Elsmarie and Dad talking to Aunt Anna on the porch. They all had serious expressions on their faces. As I walked up to them, I heard the aunt say, "Well, if you feel that way, then maybe you should write a letter to him and tell him how you feel."

"That's a good idea," Elsmarie said. "Because he has to know how hurtful his words were to us." She was really mad. I wondered what was said before I got there.

I knew that Elsmarie would do a great job with the letter. "We're going," I said.

"Don't you think you should stay?" Elsmarie looked at me impatiently. "What about all these people? You should stay," she said.

"I can't stay any longer." Sherm led me away from everyone and put me in the car and then he got in behind the wheel, backed out of the long driveway and drove away. He held me tight against his side and let the miles slip away under the wheels of the car. He didn't talk and he didn't play the radio. He just drove. He did everything exactly right.

I didn't talk to anyone for the next couple of days, then Elsmarie called on the second morning after the funeral. "Eileen, we've got to go pack up Mom's things. Dad can't do it... he's really in bad shape. I'm worried about him."

"Is he drinking?" I asked.

"I haven't seen him take a drop through this whole thing, but I've never seen him this way. He's acting like he always did on Sunday mornings, you know, shaky and guilty but usually that's worn off by the time 'The Ed Sullivan Show' comes on at night, but there's no end to this. He seems to be so depressed that I'm worried. Let's go get Mom and Dad's things out of the house for him. I'm telling you Dad can't do it; he says he'll never be able to go upstairs in that house again after seeing Mom dead up there."

"I'm not sure I'm up to it, either," I said. I didn't know much about feelings, but something told me that this was going to be bad. However, I didn't have much choice that I could see.

"We have to be strong, Eileen," Elsmarie's voice sounded strong, but then she was always strong. "I'll pick you up in a little while, George wants me to put these kids down for a nap before I go so he can rest."

Elsmarie unlocked the door of the house with the key she had gotten from Dad. The first thing we noticed walking in the kitchen was the little pan of soup Dad had fixed for Mom that last morning was still sitting on the stove and the bowl was on the center of the table. Elsmarie grabbed those dishes and put them in the sink, turning on the hot water tap to clean them. That done, there wasn't a thing out of place. The sun shone through the thin cotton print curtains onto the worn linoleum beneath our feet. Elsmarie shook her head as she led us through the small, sparsely furnished living room to the stairway. I followed her slowly up the stairs where at the top we were in Mom and Dad's bedroom and the place where she died.

I looked over to their bed and then turned away. The sheet and spread had been pulled back way to the footboard on the side of the bed and the imprint of her head was still on her pillow. Mom's white slip had been laid carefully across the footboard of the bed. We stood there looking around and wiping tears from our eyes with the heels of our hands. "Let's get started," Elsmarie said gruffly. She opened the closet door while I started opening dresser drawers. The dresser had been beautiful once with dark wood and carved ornamental trim, but the finish was dull and scratched now and the drawers did not open smoothly.

"There's not much of anything in these drawers, Elsmarie." I pulled out a few pairs of worn panties and one bra, there were some old stockings and a few of her cherished hankies that had been carefully ironed and folded. A pink cotton summer housecoat was hung on a knob on the side of the mirror. I looked over at Elsmarie who was holding the dresses from the closet in one hand.

"Look at this!" she said angrily. "How in the hell is this possible?" She tossed the dresses on the bed, "Count them, what are there, six dresses there? And that same coat that she's been wearing for years that someone gave her from the hospital... it's too damn

165

big for her anyway!" The tears flowed down her cheeks and she sat down on the bed, putting her head in her hands. I went over to her and put my hand on her shoulder to try to calm her from shaking. She looked up and asked, "How can a woman live to be fifty years old and not have anything more than this, Eileen?" I shook my head. I didn't have an answer. We carefully folded up the dresses and the underwear, picked up her pocketbook and her shoes and we put all of Mom's worldly goods into three grocery bags and took them from the little house.

Out in Elsmarie's car, we sat for a minute and used up the rest of the tissues that were stuffed in our purses. "I'm carrying toilet paper in my purse just like Mom always did." Elsmarie smiled through her tears. "You know why she always carried that big wad in her purse, don't you?"

I shook my head no and blew my nose again.

"They didn't stock any toilet paper in the patient bathrooms... Mom said it was because some of the patients would use a whole roll at a time and stop up the toilets so they rationed it out to each person and they had to carry it around with them."

I looked over at her and said, "Mom never told me anything about the way it was for her at the hospital... she told you lots of things. You told me that one time she even talked about how awful the shock treatments were."

"She told me because I asked her about it, besides, you were her baby and she was always trying to protect you so she wouldn't have told you anything but good things." Elsmarie opened her purse back up and looked in and then said, "Here's the letter I wrote to dear Captain Swanson about the funeral. Read it and see what you think."

Elsmarie took the letter from the envelope and handed it to me to read:

Dear Captain Swanson:
We requested that you officiate at the funeral of our family member because we believed that she would have desired to have the clergy from the Salvation Army. The reason we believe she would have chosen you is because she was very loyal to the Army. You spoke of her as though she was a

stranger off the street, stating that you 'hoped that she was saved' and 'you didn't know if she was a Christian.'

We do not understand how you could not have known about her loyalty to the Salvation Army and about the times she walked to the Army to attend the Ladies Aid, often in very cold weather, because it was so meaningful to her. Don't you have a responsibility to at least talk to the family of the deceased person to try to learn something about her? If you had talked to anyone who bothered to become acquainted with Irene Sandquist, you would have learned that she was definitely a Christian and one of the kindest people we know. It is unfortunate that more people in your congregation cannot follow her example and avoid judging and criticizing others without knowing the circumstances under which they are forced to live. Enclosed please find your check for services rendered.

Sincerely yours,
The family of the late Irene Sandquist

XVII

Living without Mom should have been easy: After all, I'd never really had her anyway. Some people see their mothers, or at least talk to them, every day and it might seem that it would be harder for them to fill that void left in their lives at the death of those ever-present parents. I had learned to go months without seeing Mom, and when I got to my teenage years, I learned to avoid thinking about her at all while I lived in my fantasy world with my imaginary mom. Many years later, I would learn from a counselor that not only did it matter terribly that she was missing from my life, but that I was so traumatized over the fact that she was taken away from me that my feelings were frozen. It would take nearly twenty years of living with the grief, guilt and anger over the way things were with us before I would begin to deal with those strong feelings in a healthy way. Years in which I searched on my own for the answers before I ever knew the questions

How could any of it have happened the way it did? I spent a long time unsure which was worse: the guilt and self-loathing I felt about my own neglectful and sometimes abusive behavior towards my mother; or the anger that bordered on rage that I felt towards my father, and the state hospital. Part of the time I was even angry at her, "Why didn't she fight for her rights?" I would ask myself, or God, or whoever listens to the anguished cries that are spoken, usually in a darkened room while others sleep. In some ways, her influence over me was greater after her death than it was when she was living; everything I did seemed to be an action towards her, or against her. I was either proving to the world how unlike her I was by being self-sufficient and showing how I could control my surroundings, or how like her I was with my ability to get by with only bare essentials for myself. Self-knowledge, and the ability to lead a reasonable and rational lifestyle were not within my grasp. It would be many years before I could begin to find anything close to peace, and the answers came through many different sources. It was a journey, often only of the mind, but sometimes there was actual travel involved and new friends to shed a little light. It was more than a year after Mom's death when I met the first person who helped me understand at least in part what Mom might have gone through. I met her through a job I had taken as a waitress in a lunch counter. I was reluctant to tell my sister about my plan that winter afternoon.

"There's something I've been thinking about doing," I said cautiously. "Do you remember my telling you about that nice older lady, Mrs. Johnson, who comes to Grants to have lunch on Fridays?" Elsmarie looked blank, so I just went on, "Well, she goes to West Palm Beach, Florida, every winter for a few weeks and stays in a rooming house. She's related to one of our cousins' husbands."

Elsmarie looked at me intently. "Yeah, I remember you mentioning something about her."

I looked away from Elsmarie's gaze and said, "She's leaving on the Greyhound Bus in two weeks and she said I might like to go with her sometime." I spoke quickly. "I think I might go with her."

"Is she going to pay your way?" she asked sarcastically. "Just what are you going to do for money?"

"Our tax refund will be here by then... I'm going to tell Sherm I want half of the tax refund." I stared down at Elsmarie's worn linoleum as I spoke.

There wasn't a sound for a long time, then Elsmarie said, "So you're just going to walk away from everyone, just like that." She got up and started doing something at the sink. "Does Dad know?"

I knew she was mad at me, and I suddenly felt mad too. "The last time I talked to Dad was when he came to my house at eleven o'clock at night, drunk and then he actually started talking about Mom to me, you know, like he used to." She still had her back to me. "I said, 'don't you dare come around here drunk and start talking about Mom to me! She's dead!' I told him, 'have some respect for someone who's dead!' Well, he got all huffy then and said, 'So now everything was my fault, I suppose!' I finally just told him that if he was going to keep sitting there and arguing and saying bad things about Mom, then he didn't need to come back! I hated telling him that, but I can't listen to it anymore now!" I got up and walked over by her window and looked out at the snow in the yard.

Elsmarie said, "He did that here, too and I told him the same thing. I don't know why he went back to drinking, but I can't take it anymore either, when he does that." She didn't sound as mad at me anymore. For a long time, neither of us spoke and then she seemed to brighten a little, "Well, you won't ever go to Florida anyway. There's no way that you'll ever be able to leave Sherm."

"I can leave Sherm," I said and sat back at the table with her. "He's getting ready to leave me, anyway, I can tell by the way he acts. I guess I'm like you, I'm just tired of the whole thing and I don't think I care anymore." Two weeks later, Sherm, Elsmarie and Dad waited with me at the bus station in Jamestown with expressions of surprise on their faces and watched while I climbed aboard behind Mrs. Johnson and we waved goodbye to our families as the bus lurched and pulled out of the station. I just wanted to escape from everything.

Mrs. Johnson was eighty-two years old. She was a little woman, slightly bent-over with short gray hair, a broad smile and bright blue eyes that sparkled with mischief. She had told me about her nine grown children and how each one of them had made her feel welcome to live with them, but that she much preferred the independent life and insisted on keeping her small apartment in Jamestown and going for her winter retreats to West Palm Beach, Florida. "I'll get a job when I get down there," she said. "I'll find some poor old thing who can't get around well enough on her own ·anymore and I'll work as her companion for a while, and before I go, I'll help her find someone to take my place and then I'll go back home."

"Do you miss your family when you're away from them, Mrs. Johnson?" I asked her after we had been traveling on the highway long enough for the late afternoon sun of our departure had become pitch black.

"Lord, no, Honey," she said, "I love my family and I'll be glad to see them when I get home, but one of the reasons I go to Florida is to get away from them." She laughed. "Young people today think that old folks like me want to be entertained by them all the time. I like to be alone sometimes. It's peaceful and I can think."

"How long ago did your husband pass away?" I asked and I hoped I wasn't bringing back the pain of his death by asking.

She thought a minute and then said, "Why, it's been more than twelve years now since he died."

"I'm sorry that he died, I guess you were married a very long time. Do you still miss him?"

She was quiet again, and then she said, "We were married more than fifty years." She paused and then she looked at me. The full moon looked like a large melon above the trees and its light made her face seem young and smooth. "I was faithful to him and I was a good wife." She paused again. "But I was not sad to see the old coot die." And then she laughed. I laughed, too, right out loud at her answer. She went on to say, "I don't mean to speak ill of the dead, but that man ruled all of us, me and every one of our nine children, with an iron hand. And he drank liquor every chance he got and had more women than either one of us could count during our fifty years."

"But you stayed with him," I said softly. "My dad drank and my mother stayed with him, too. I don't understand why she didn't leave him."

"I didn't have a choice." Mrs. Johnson turned to look at me; "Women didn't have choices in my day. You got married for better or worse, and if it turned out to be for worse… well, that's just the way it was." She leaned back in her seat. "The men had all the jobs, all the money and all the power. I can tell you, if there had been any way for me to make it on my own and keep my children, then I would have left in a minute."

"I guess my dad had all the power over my mother, too," I said.

"Of course he did!" she said quickly. "Your mother's generation didn't have any more choices than we did. Women didn't even start to work outside of the homes until just the past few years. You have to be able to earn a living if you want to have any control over your own life, so not only could women not leave their husbands, but they had to try to keep the old goats happy enough so they wouldn't desert the home and leave the family penniless."

"It sounds pretty awful."

"Well, it wasn't bad for everyone. There are some fine men and they are faithful and sober and decent to their wives and children; a good man actually respects and admires his wife for what she does in the home. But, if you get a lemon, well... the only chance the woman has for a little happiness is to outlive the old fool, which is what I was lucky enough to do. Now, I get his social security check every month and I'm able to do whatever I want, and it feels good."

After a while I said, "My mother wasn't lucky, she died first."

Mrs. Johnson reached over and patted my hand, "I'm real sorry to hear that, Honey. I guess you'll just have to find enough happiness for both of you. You know, you don't have to be stuck just because she was. The world is finally getting to be a little better place for women. You don't have to stick with a man who treats you badly. Some of them act like they don't have the sense they were born with. Well, I'll keep still and not go on about it." Mrs. Johnson let her voice trail off.

We shared a room in a nice rooming house in West Palm Beach for seven weeks and then one day I came home from my job at Kress Department Store to find her packing. She greeted me with her usual smile and bright eyes. "It's time to go home," she said. "My job's over. The old lady's daughter came back from her trip and they don't need me anymore." She sat down on her bed and said, "I need to keep busy so I guess I'll go back home, but I'll miss you, you've been a good roommate."

"I'll miss you, too," I said. "I don't know what I would have done without you."

"Well, you would have been just fine! Just look how well you've done!" She had a great smile. "I was a little worried that first week or so that you were going to hop right back on the bus and go back home, but aren't you glad you didn't?" She finished her packing while she spoke, "Just look at you! You found yourself a job right away and you go to work every day and manage your money. You've put on some weight and you're tanned and healthy-looking. You're going to be just fine." Her eyes took on that mischievous look. "I don't know if you've noticed, but there's a couple of those young men visiting Mrs. Blinn's son down on the sun porch who have their eyes on you." She closed her suitcase and locked it and picked up her purse. "Choose wisely, Honey. Don't take the first man who comes along." Mrs. Johnson gave me a quick hug and said, "I'm going downstairs to call a taxi. My bus leaves soon. Let's say goodbye here. I'll see you again, someday."

The following week, Sherm arrived unannounced in an old green station wagon that gasped and sputtered before it died as he pulled up to the curb in front of Blinn's Rooming House. It took us three days to find a junk yard that was willing to come and pick it up for us. Sherm found a job at a service station in town and we just picked up where we had left off.

XVIII

When you're very young, time seems to stand still, and waiting patiently for something to happen can be the greatest pain of all. But, even for the young, weeks turn into months and months to years and sometimes, in the process, we do get what we want. My first child burst into the world within a year after Sherm and his old green car arrived in West Palm Beach. We returned home and moved to a little house in the country with our small son. His birth marked the end of a pregnancy that was full of nightmares about miscarriages, stillbirths, and small white caskets. Having a healthy baby left only the first year of his life to continue having nightmares about crib deaths, spinal meningitis and horrible accidents. A second son three years later left me somewhat less traumatized than the first, but I was still happier when he also got through the baby stages. Lois, the neighbor, would stop by to visit now and then and hold baby Scott. Her children were pretty well grown and she'd look down at the peaceful baby longingly and say, "Don't you wish they could just be babies forever?" I thought she must be out of her mind to want that worry forever.

Elsmarie put up a good fight to keep George from leaving every couple of months until he started getting violent with her. One night, they invited us over for a cook out and George just kept drinking until he was so smashed that he decided to take off in the car and when Elsmarie tried to stop him, he hit her and slammed her leg with the car door and drove off, leaving her by the side of the road. It was the end for their marriage.

Dad had remarried shortly after I moved to Florida to a woman who was a few years older than he. She had never been married and was, of course, very set in her ways. She had started working in a factory during World War II, like many women did when their husbands were in the military, but most of them gave up their jobs when their husbands came back from the service. Women who didn't have husbands just kept working. She was retired by the time she met Dad and owned a nice older two-story home and a late model car. Dad even had a little area in the basement where he could do some woodworking projects; something he hadn't been able to do since he and Mom had that nice house up on Oak Street that was pictured in the old photo albums.

Dad retired as soon as he turned sixty-two and then he gave up drinking. Before long, he was turning out gifts for all of us from his basement workshop. Jewelry boxes for Elsmarie and me, toy storage boxes for all the kids with their names etched on top. They rented a cottage at the lake one summer and Dad took his grandchildren by their hands and led them to the end of the dock where they would all sit while he showed them how to bait a fish hook and the best way to pull in a fish once you had him caught. He performed these simple acts of love quietly and softly and there was something in his eyes that I didn't want to see because it was painful.

You didn't have to be in the company of Dad and Gertie very long to learn who was the boss in their little household. He always seemed nervous around her and he made it a point to never disappoint her. He used to visit me sometimes on Saturday mornings. I'd put the coffee on and we'd make small talk about the weather, politics, or the price of gasoline and maybe he'd hold his grandsons on his lap for a while. As soon as it got to be about eleven o'clock on those morning visits he would begin to fidget and start watching the clock and it wouldn't be long before he would say, "Well, I better get going. She puts lunch on the table right at noon."

One time I got brave and said, "Call her up and tell her that I'm fixing lunch for you today."

"Oh no, I can't do that," he said, getting up and slipping into his jacket. "She wouldn't like that at all."

Neither Dad nor I had ever mentioned Mom since that night years ago when I told him to never say anything bad about her again in my presence, but I couldn't keep still anymore about this. "You know, Dad," I tried not to sound as hurt as I really felt, "Maybe if you had showed Mom just half the consideration that you show to Gertie, then things would have been better for all of us… maybe she would have had some of the simple things in life that she was denied."

He stood by the door with his hand on the knob and looked down at the floor. "Well, maybe I know that," he said softly. "Maybe I'm just trying to do some thing right now." And having said that, he walked out.

Just about the time you start thinking that there will be some easy answers to a question, then things get more complicated. Dad had worked very well for some time as someone to blame for the tragedy of Mom's life, until he became ill himself and found redemption and what certainly appeared as forgiveness from God.

None of us knew that time with Dad would be growing short, nor did we know just how graciously he would be redeemed for his past discretions. There were some good times to come with Elsmarie's remarriage to a wonderful man named Michael. My sister had tried her best to salvage her marriage to George and he had continued to abuse her every attempt at a reasonable and nurturing relationship until she was forced to throw in the towel and apply for a divorce. Perhaps as a reward for trying so hard to succeed in that marriage, Michael came along and they fell in love. It was a long courtship and a beautiful wedding ceremony where Dad got to wear a tuxedo and escort his daughter down the aisle in a beautiful church wedding. It was a wonderful occasion that we all got to share... well, not everyone. "I wish Mom was here," said my sister, who was a beautiful and happy bride.

"Me too." I nodded slowly in agreement. I was amazed how an expensive gown and a professional hairdo can change someone's looks. Still bound by years of tradition, Elsmarie's gown was off-white, rather than true white because of her previous marriages. Everything was perfect; the service, the reception later in the hotel ballroom and they even left in a rain of rice for a honeymoon in the Bahama Islands.

There was a knot of uneasiness that started to form just prior to Elsmarie's wedding and it became a point of discussion between us after she returned from her honeymoon. "I'm worried about Dad," I said to her over the phone. "He doesn't look good... and have you noticed how swollen his stomach is lately?"

"Yes, and I asked him about it already. He said it's nothing to worry about," she answered. There was a long silence.

"I'm still worried," I said. "I'm going to talk with him about it too."

As the weeks passed, Dad kept looking worse and Elsmarie and I kept trying to talk him into going to a doctor. He had gotten to the point where he was annoyed at out insistence, so we had to be cautious. One day, he and Gertie visited and I looked at his ashen face and his stomach that protruded more than ever and I caught him wincing as if in pain and applying pressure to the lower part of his stomach with the heel of his hand and I said, "I can't take this anymore!" The words were coming from somewhere inside of me. "You are sick! And I can't stand to see you like this. Please go to the doctor."

"I can't talk to you or your sister anymore!" he said, sounding frustrated, more than angry. "All either one of you want to talk about is going to the doctor. You two have to let up on me!" Again, Gertie said nothing. They left shortly after that conversation.

Two days later, Dad called and said, "I just thought I'd tell you that I'm going to the doctor on Monday."

He kept his appointment and then things happened fast. Within the week he was in the hospital scheduled for surgery on his colon. Elsmarie, Gertie and I paced the floor of the waiting room on Dad's floor for several hours. After what seemed to be forever, Dr. Cho came to talk with us. Dad had waited too long to see the doctor. "The news isn't good," he said. The cancer has spread and we were unable to get it all. We have performed a colostomy and we will give him chemotherapy to try to stop the advancement of the cancer."

"How long does he have?" I'm not sure which one of us put words to the question that pressed on all of our minds.

"Maybe six months... who knows?" he said softly. "If the chemotherapy does good work, then maybe two years."

The plan was to get him back on his feet after surgery so he could go home and return for short periods of time for his chemo treatments. The idea was to give him some quality time so he could have some enjoyment in the time he had remaining. It didn't happen that way. Dad didn't get back on his feet and the time he had remaining became a time when the ordinary things in life stood still and made way for heroes.

Sherm held me up me for those next months. I never had to think about what I would have done without him. I needed to be with Dad. I went to the hospital everyday when Sherm came home from work, He walked in the door and I walked out and we'd stop for a quick embrace and a passing kiss that sometimes landed on chin or cheek as I hurried to the hospital room kept dark so Dad's pounding headaches could be eased. Nothing seemed to help his pain, nor the projectile vomiting that came after the daily doses of chemotherapy. The pain medications kept him nearly unconscious, but he had moments when he was lucid and he would beg to be taken home. Each day, I'd go in hopeful for a sign that the treatment was working, but would find instead that the disease had left his body more ravaged than the day before. The doctor said that the disease had spread to his lungs and would soon overtake his brain. There was no hope. Seeing our father in this state became normal in some insane way and we found that we could joke with the nurses, read the newspaper and discuss the weather next to the dying man who had become nothing more than the shell of a very large man who was our father.

During those long evenings sitting by his bed, memories buried from long ago came back. I was being carried on Dad's shoulders around the fire station and sitting on big red trucks. Then I was getting up on Easter Sunday mornings to bowls of cooked eggs chopped up with melted butter and toast that had been made crisp in the oven. There was a time that was so long ago that it was hard to tell if my memories were wishes when life wasn't scary and lonely. There was a toy wooden telephone that was brought up from a basement workshop and a large stuffed doll as big as I was. There was a trip somewhere with Elsmarie and me riding in the back seat covered with paper dolls while Dad and Mom sat in the front side by side.

It was the day before Easter Sunday, but there was no time to color eggs with two little boys, or plan special outfits. Dad had been sinking lower and lower until there was no response from him. He had stopped waking at intervals to accept a sip of water from the bedside cup. I left at nine that night to try to find some candy to fill the baskets for the children, but had barely arrived back when the hospital called me back. "We don't think he'll last the night," the charge nurse said over the phone. So this was going to be it.

The hospital had notified Gertie and it was my job to call Elsmarie, who was living about four hours away where her husband's jobsite was located. Having done that, I went to the hospital for what was to be the last time. As soon as I got to his floor, the nurse said, "He's deep in a coma. He's not feeling anything and his blood pressure is very low." She was very kind in her manner. "Is your sister coming? We called your stepmother, but I don't think she's coming tonight."

I went in and looked at Dad's still form on the bed. The room was dark except for the light shining in through the door from the hall. I stood and watched him labor to move his chest up and down and then I heard him speak in a clear voice. I hadn't heard him speak in weeks. It startled me and I looked over at him and his eyes were still tightly shut, but he was speaking to someone, "Yes... I know that," he said, "but doesn't everyone make mistakes?" I wanted to move closer to him, but I found myself moving back as he went on. I had an overwhelming feeling that I was witnessing something that was not intended for me and that I was an intruder, but I couldn't move to leave. He went on to say, "I am very sorry that I did that." There was silence and I looked over and even though his eyes were still closed, he had an expression that suggested he was listening to someone that only he could hear. And then he actually nodded slightly and said, "I wish I could do that." And then he was silent again.

I waited from over by the window to see if there would be any more words, and after a period of silence, I walked over to him cautiously and looked for anything else that might be different. There didn't appear to be any change physically and he looked as he did when I came in; like a man who was deep in a coma. I went out to the nurse and said, "Could you come in and check his vital signs again?" She looked at me with a questioning expression and came behind me. She put the blood pressure cuff on Dad and pumped the little bulb and checked the meter shaking her head.

"There's no difference," she said.

179

"Do people in comas usually talk?" I asked without trying to explain what just happened.

"If he talks, that would be a miracle right now, Honey, because that would mean he had come out of his coma." She smiled kindly at me, "He's not going to talk anymore, Honey. His blood pressure is so low that it doesn't register. It won't be long now."

I remembered a conversation that Elsmarie and Gertie had one day about who we would get as a minister when the end came. We agreed to call Dad's childhood friend, Ray, who had become a Methodist minister rather late in life. I went down the hall to the pay phones and called him. I didn't even think about the fact that it was only five o'clock in the morning. All I knew was that Dad had spoken to someone; maybe he wanted to speak to a minister.

"Sure," came a kind, but sleepy voice over the phone. "I remember your dad. Golly, I'm sorry to hear about him being so sick." He cleared his throat and then he said in a strong voice, "I'll get dressed now and I'll be down."

I went back to Dad's room to check on him. There was no change. It seemed like he was hardly breathing at all and his hand felt cold. I tried to cover it up as best I could, but it was taped to the IV board and the hose kept getting in the way. I allowed some time for Dad's friend to get ready and then I went down to the elevators to wait for him. Night had given way to a bright sunlit blue sky as I looked out the window to the road below. Everywhere there were signs of life; down on the street below the traffic thickened and the elevators brought carloads of nurses to the fourth floor. The elevator doors would open and fresh-faced nurses would bid each other a good day and go off in different directions in pairs or groups of three and four to work. I watched the lights on the wall above the elevator and listened for the distinctive sound it made when it stopped on our floor, anticipating the arrival of the man who would minister to my dying father's soul. And on one of the stops, a tall man emerged in a brown suit and blue tie. He was very tall and on the slim side with blue eyes and a smile that lit up the dreary hallway. He looked at me questioningly, "Eileen, is that you?" he asked easily. I went over and took his outstretched and thanked him for coming.

"Dad's in Room 410, Ray. I'll wait here." I remembered back

when Grandma Stewart had passed away and she wanted to see the minister alone. I didn't much want to be there anyway. I stayed by the elevators, realizing that Elsmarie would be coming any minute, and probably Gertie as well. It wasn't long before they all got off the elevator. "The minister is with Dad," I said. I looked at Elsmarie and then at Gertie and said, "I called Ray, the one we talked about, he's down there now." They nodded and sat down on the cushioned window seat that was at the elevators.

"How's Dad?" Elsmarie asked.

I shook my head. "Not good." I wanted to tell her about Dad talking, but I didn't want to tell it in front of Gertie. I was afraid it would make her mad that she hadn't been the one to hear him. She didn't like it that I spent so much time with him as it was. She used to come in during the daytime visiting hours, and one day I arrived before she left.

"The nurses tell me that you come here at night." She sounded really mad about it. "Well, I can't be out all hours of the night!"

"I know," I answered that day, "I know you're here during the day. I can't come during the day so this way he doesn't have to be alone." So I wasn't about to tell her that I knew something she didn't.

Gertie wasn't very patient about anything. She waited in the hall with us for about five minutes and then she said, "I'm going down to the room." Just as she said that, Ray came out the double doors that led into the floor where Dad's room was and he was smiling. I introduced him to everyone.

"Carl and I had a great talk," he said, "That was as good for me as it was for him."

"You remember him, don't you?" I asked. "You were in Room 410, right?" I looked over at Elsmarie and Gertie and then we all looked at Ray. "Dad was in a deep coma when I called you this morning."

Ray just kept grinning, "Well, he's not in one now. We had a great talk…" Ray looked around at all of us and then he said, "Go on down… he's waiting for all of you. Gosh, he's just full of love." Ray wiped at tears in his eyes and then he said, "Listen, I'm going to go for a while. Peg's going to have something for me to eat, but I'll

181

come back tonight."

Ray was true to his word and we found Dad just as he said we would: Sitting up in bed and full of love for all of us. He hugged us all and repeated over and over his gratitude to God that he had some more time with his family. I began to wonder if this was real, or a return to my imaginary father of my early teenage years. Over the next few weeks, Ray and Dad embarked on a Spiritual journey together that kept them occupied for long periods of time every evening. After their evening talk, Ray would come out of Dad's room with his wide grin and say, "Golly, this is better for me than it is for your dad," or, "I told Carl he needs to get well and he and I will take this story and tour the countryside with it, but you know that no one will believe it."

God gave us just three more months with Dad before it was time to make the final trip with him to the hospital. Elsmarie and I kept a bedside vigil for one week and then Dad passed away quietly at a time when we had just stepped outside of his room. It was over and we, now orphaned at twenty-nine and thirty-four respectively, were left to make whatever sense we could of the tragedy of our parents' lives. There were no more bad guys left to blame. How could we go on blaming Dad for the tragedy of Mom's life when God so clearly had forgiven him? The question of what to do with all of it remained. I was sad because my sons, Sherm, Jr. and Scott, would never know their grandmother, and now, they were denied forever the company of their grandfather as well.

Dysfunctional families produce dysfunctional children who grow up to be dysfunctional adults. Over the years I caused as much pain as I endured, even though I learned everything I could about alcoholism, its effects on the family and the inner workings of a state mental hospital. I read books, attended lectures, earned college degrees and became a counselor. I went through counseling myself and made brave attempts to unload my anger and grief over my mother through a painful process that led me to experience my own feelings for perhaps the first time in my life. Still, peace eluded me.

One hot summer afternoon, I stood outside under the maple tree and watched my fifteen-year-old son trying to start our old lawn mower. He was struggling with so many things since he became a teenager and our relationship was very strained. I didn't know how to talk to him anymore. I watched him pull the cord over and over trying to get the motor to catch and at one point he reached his hand up to brush away something in his eye. It might have been an insect, or a bead of sweat, or a tear, and I saw how vulnerable he was. He didn't know I was watching him and at that moment I felt such overwhelming love and compassion for him that I couldn't stop the flow of tears. It was at that very moment that I realized that God wept for me, just as I wept for my son.

God was not enjoying my misfortune and He did not enjoy my mother's pain while she was here on earth and was certainly not the cause of any of it anymore than I was enjoying Scott's pain. Suddenly it all became clear. We are all children of God, and as long as we dwell on earth we are subject to the illnesses and misfortunes that come with life. God couldn't keep my family from pain anymore than I could keep Scott from pain. God did what He could; He walked with me. I could see that He had surely walked with my mother, and were it not for the Grace of God, I could be in a horrible place today. I was healthy, educated and creative, and I had two wonderful sons. I finally had the answer I had been searching for now that I finally knew the truth about God. There could never be a promise that that there would be no more pain. God doesn't decode state laws, society's laws, and who will be stricken with disease, but He can promise to be there by our sides, if we'll let Him.

What I learned about God helped me to forgive my family and myself and made closure possible for me. I knew that I should look past the problems that my parents had that caused us all so much pain, and look, instead, for the goods that we inherited from them. We needed to focus on those fine qualities that each one possessed and passed on to us, their children. They each had many. I learned that I probably inherited my desire and ability to write from my father. Not only was he a writer as we learned at the end of his life, but we have since learned that his mother, our farmor, wrote as well. I also inherited his dry sense of humor and a love of woodworking. Underneath all of his alcoholic-induced veneer, he was a deeply sensitive and loving man.

As I give my mother her rightful place as the matriarch of our family, I can easily point to her qualities. She was a loving and responsible wife and mother. I inherited her strong sense of duty and her desire for things to be done correctly. I inherited her love of music, particularly opera, and I also enjoy dancing. Mother loved to knit and crochet and could have easily mastered other crafts as well. While I could never compete with her in knitting, I enjoy crafts and artwork. Mother had a strong sense of right and wrong and she believed that we should a speak well of others and be loyal to family. I'm not as good as she was about that, but I'm working on it. I now know that my mother had a profound influence on my life and, therefore, the lives of others even though she was a woman of limited means.

*